# What If Someone I Know Is Gay?

### Answers to Questions About Gay and Lesbian People

## by Eric Marcus

*PSS!*
PRICE STERN SLOAN

Copyright © 2000 by Eric Marcus.
All rights reserved. Published by Price Stern Sloan,
a division of Penguin Putnam Books for Young Readers, New York.
Printed in the United States of America.
Published simultaneously in Canada.
No part of this publication may be reproduced, stored in any
retrieval system,or transmitted, in any form or by any means,
electronic, mechanical, photocopying,recording, or otherwise, without
the prior written permission of the publisher.

*Library of Congress Catalog Card Number : 00-108447*

ISBN 0-8431-7611-3 (pb)  A B C D E F G H I J
ISBN 0-8431-7612-1(GB)  A B C D E F G H I J

PLUGGED IN! ™ is a trademark of Penguin Putnam Inc.
PSS! ® is a registered trademark of Penguin Putnam Inc.

At last, a book for Rachel—E. M.

# Acknowledgements

I am very grateful to my publisher Jane O'Connor for suggesting this book; to Joel Fotinos for suggesting that I was the one to write it; to my agent Joy Harris, for encouraging me to do it; and to the staff at Price Stern Sloan for seeing this book through from beginning to end, including Emily Sollinger, Jennifer Frantz, Ranse Ransone, Lisa Donovan, and Carol Rosenberg. Thank you all.

Thank you also to the many people who contributed their questions and thoughts and/or offered their help, support, and/or advice, including Doug Aucoin, Dr. Betty Berzon, Sally Bourrie, Duffie Cohen, Dr. M. S. Frommer, Dr. Richard Hersh, Rachel Katz, Leslie Longenbough, Cynthia Lubow, Lewis and Maureen Marcus, Ryan Marcus, Yona Zeldis McDonough, Stephen Milioti, Stuart Schear, Jonathan Schwartz, and Chris Tuttle.

Many, many thanks to those who read all or part of the manuscript and offered their valuable advice and comments. These include Dr. Leslie Bogen, Kate Chieco, Cynthia Smith DiPalma, Arlene Eisenberg, Laura and John Foster, Kevin Jennings, Beth Karpfinger, Heidi Katz, Nancy Kokolj, Chris Lord, Rochelle Lefkowitz, Mynette Marcus, Brian McNaught, Pamela Wilson, and Penelope Tzougros.

And, as always, for his love and unwavering support, thank you to my H.B., Barney Karpfinger, who always seems to know better than I that I can get it done.

# table of contents

# Introduction

Everyone knows someone who is gay: a sister or brother, aunt or uncle, parent, grandparent, teacher, or friend. Or, perhaps, you're gay yourself or you think that you might be. Of course, a lot of people don't realize that they know someone who is gay or lesbian because many gay men and women keep it a secret. Why? That's a good question and it's just one of many that you'll find answered in this book.

The way I see it, there is no such thing as a stupid question. Well, with one exception. The only stupid question is the one you don't ask. And when it comes to the subject of gay and lesbian people and gay issues, there are a lot of questions that never get asked and a lot of answers that never get offered. I think we'd all be a lot better off if kids could feel okay asking questions and had someplace where they could find the commonsense answers they're looking for. That's why I've written *What If Someone I Know Is Gay?*

What you'll find here are lots of questions: some very obvious, some not so obvious, and some that you might even think are stupid. Most of the questions I've included have been asked of me over the years both in my role as an author and in my personal life. Some questions come directly from kids who have written to me or e-mailed me after reading one of my other books or responded to my e-mail request for question suggestions. And some were contributed by friends, family, and colleagues after I told them I'd been asked to write a book about gay stuff for young people.

In offering answers, I've done my best to be direct. Sometimes, to help illustrate a point I'm trying to make, I include stories from my own life or from people I've met and talked to during the past fifteen years. Occasionally, I also offer my own opinions. I don't speak for any organizations, political parties, or religious groups. I speak for myself and no one else.

At the end of the book, you'll find lots of resource information that I hope will be of help to those of you who are looking for more than what you'll find in these few pages. After all, this book is really just a brief introduction to a huge and complicated subject about which many people still have strong and differing opinions.

Just a note about the people in the book who I identify by name. All adults who asked that I use their names are identified by their full names. For all young people, I've used only first names and I've changed all of these names to maintain the privacy of the people who were kind enough to allow me to interview them. Most of the young people I talked to wanted me to use their real first names or their full names, but I prefer that they remain anonymous. That's mostly because I don't want to be responsible for whatever unintended impact public exposure could have on their lives.

For the young people I interviewed who are gay and not public about it, I've also changed some identifying characteristics in addition to changing their names.

If there are questions you would like to see included in the next edition of *What If Someone I Know Is Gay?* or if there are questions you think I could have done a better job answering, let me know. You can write to me: Eric Marcus c/o Price Stern Sloan / 345 Hudson Street/ 14th Floor/ New York, NY 10014, or you can e-mail me directly at ericmarcus@aol.com.

# chapter 1

# The Basic Stuff

### What does "gay" mean?

**B**oys and girls who grow up to have strong feelings of sexual attraction for people of the same gender are called "gay" or "homosexual." ("Gay" or "homosexual" can refer to both men and women, although many women who are gay prefer to be called "lesbian.") Men and women who have strong feelings of sexual attraction for people of the other gender are called "straight" or "heterosexual." And those people who have strong feelings of sexual attraction for people of both genders are called "bisexual."

## How do you become gay?

Simple answer—you can't *become* gay, just like you can't *become* heterosexual. You are what you are.

This is how it works: All of us have feelings of sexual attraction. Most of us have these feelings for people of the other gender—boys for girls, girls for boys. Some of us have these feelings for people of the same gender—boys for boys, girls for girls. And some people have feelings of sexual attraction for both the same gender and the other gender.

For example, when Mae was ten years old, she already knew she was different from most of her classmates. "A lot of the girls in elementary school were boy crazy. I knew that I wasn't, but I pretended to be like everyone else."

No one knows exactly how we come by our feelings of sexual attraction in the first place, but whether we're born with them or develop them in the early years of life, they are a gift—from God, from nature, from our genes—and they can make us feel very good and sometimes very confused.

As we enter our teen years, these feelings of attraction grow stronger and we often find ourselves both emotionally and physically—or sexually—attracted to another person. That was Mae's experience. By the time she was thirteen, her feelings of sexual attraction were clear. "When I was thirteen I admitted it to myself. My friends were always talking about being attracted to cute guys. And I was always just attracted to girls. It was a feeling inside. I tried to be attracted to guys, but it wasn't working."

Keep in mind that human sexuality is a very complicated thing and that many people don't fit neatly into one category or another.

### What exactly are "feelings of sexual attraction?"

As we grow into adolescence and our bodies change, we begin to have strong feelings of attraction that are different from and more intense than the good feelings we might have for a relative or a friend. It is these strong feelings of sexual attraction that make us want to have a sexual relationship. For some kids these feelings begin before puberty and for others they don't come until after. These special feelings of excitement and desire are difficult to describe, but you'll know them when you experience them.

### Is being gay a choice?

I'm asked this question more often than just about any other and the answer is more complicated than a simple "no." People don't choose their feelings of sexual attraction. That's true for EVERYONE. Whether you have feelings of sexual attraction for people of the same gender, the other gender, or both, these are not feelings you have chosen. Like your eye color, skin color, or height, you don't get a choice. These feelings have chosen you. However, what you decide to do about these feelings is a matter of choice.

### Can you change your feelings?

No. When it comes to feelings of sexual attraction, no amount of hoping, praying, psychotherapy, or wishful thinking will make them go away. Unlike most gifts, when it comes to your feelings of sexual attraction, there are no exchanges and no returns. You can try to ignore your feelings, you can pretend you're not having them, but no matter what anyone says, you can't change or eliminate your feelings of sexual attraction, just as you can't change the true color of your eyes. That goes for gay people just as it does for heterosexual people.

I remember being twelve and hoping that my

I remember being twelve and hoping that my feelings for people of the same gender would change. I had a crush on my camp counselor, Ted. I didn't just like Ted. I really, really liked Ted. It's not that I wanted to have sex with him—I wasn't even certain how people had sex. But I wanted to be around Ted, I thought about him all the time, and it made me feel very good the few times he put his arm around my shoulder.

I was pretty sure that the other boys in my cabin didn't feel the way I did. For one thing, they talked a lot about Ted's girlfriend, Rebecca, a counselor in the teen division, who they thought looked amazing in a bathing suit. I could tell Rebecca was attractive, but I didn't understand what all the excitement was about. I especially didn't understand why my cabin-mates were all so interested in going on late-night raids of the girls' cabins.

At first I didn't worry about my crush on Ted and other guys, because I'd heard that some boys have these feelings and outgrow them (which is, in fact, true). But I'd also learned from other kids that these were "bad" feelings, so I was hoping I'd outgrow them fast. I figured that I would stop having crushes on male counselors and would start having crushes on girl counselors, and one day I might even want to get up in the middle of the night and crawl through the woods to the other side of camp and sneak into one of the girls' cabins. But as much as I hoped that my feelings would change, they didn't. Unlike the kids who have these feelings and outgrow them, my feelings of same gender attraction just grew stronger as I got older.

**What about the people who say they used to be gay, but now they're not? Did they really change?**

There are people who say that they used to be gay or lesbian and that they have changed or have been "cured" through prayer, through counseling, or by attending a program designed to help gay people become "ex-gays." It is true that people *can* change their behavior. But they can't change their true feelings of sexual attraction. Those feelings, no matter how hard you might try to bury them, ignore them, or convince yourself you don't have them, stay with you for as long as you live. For example, a gay man can end his relationship with another man and start having a relationship with a woman. But that doesn't mean he's suddenly developed feelings of sexual attraction for women. He still has the same feelings of sexual attraction for men that he always had. He may be trying to ignore those feelings, but they're still there.

I remember getting a letter many years ago from a former boyfriend who went through an "ex-gay" program. He wrote to me just after my first book, *The Male Couple's Guide*, was published. He told me that I could choose to change, too, just like he had. But I had long since decided to be true to myself and had no interest in trying to be something I wasn't. I knew that society would be more accepting of me if I pretended to be heterosexual, but I thought it would be better to use my energy to fight prejudice than to fight my true feelings. After all, there is nothing wrong with my feelings, so why try to pretend I don't have them?

I never heard from my old boyfriend again, but my guess is that he eventually found it impossible to change his sexual feelings for men. One way or another, I hope that he's happy.

### How can I tell if I'm gay, lesbian, or bisexual? Do you just wake up one day and discover that you're gay?

No, you don't just wake up one day and discover that you're gay, just the same as you don't wake up one day and discover that you're heterosexual. But finding a label for yourself isn't nearly as important as trying to sort out your feelings, and that can take time. For some kids, their feelings of sexual attraction are clear from an early age, as young as five or six. But for most kids, it's something they become aware of during adolescence or later, and that's the same whether you're attracted to someone of the same gender, the other gender, or both.

Jackson, who is now seventeen and is finishing his last year of high school, knew very early. "I always knew I was attracted to other guys, as far back as kindergarten. I just was. I was always curious about doing sexual stuff with other boys." Michelle also knew early, but it wasn't that she wanted to have sex with other girls. "That came later," she said. "From the time I was six I knew I was going to marry a girl. I told my parents and they said, 'That's nice, honey.' They weren't taking me seriously. I was only six. So I told them over and over again. They tried telling me I was going to marry a boy when I grew up, but I just shook my head no, 'cause I knew they were wrong."

Kevin, a high school junior in southern California, wasn't really sure of his sexual feelings until he was in his early teens, although by the time he was ten he knew he was different from most of the other boys. "But I didn't have a word for it," he told me. "I just knew. When the girls and boys started to interact, I felt totally out of place. It didn't make sense to me."

Jennifer, a nineteen-year-old college sophomore, found herself attracted to other girls at her Catholic high school. "I looked at girls and saw them as really attractive," she said, "and I wanted to be with them in more ways than just friends. I was sexually attracted to them." But Jennifer was confused by her feelings. She explained, "You're taught in society to go after the opposite sex, to date the opposite sex. I thought I was going to be a part of that. It finally took meeting another girl who was gay and talking to her about what it was like to be gay for me to realize I wasn't going to do what society told me. That was just a few months ago. And now I know for sure I don't want to pretend to be someone else."

For many people, the pressure "to go after the opposite sex" keeps them from recognizing or understanding their true feelings. They want to be like everyone else. They don't want to feel left out and alone and they don't want to have romantic and/or sexual feelings that some people think are bad. Given these circumstances, many kids and teenagers need time and the experiences of growing up to sort out and accept what they really feel.

### Are people who are bisexual attracted to men and women in the same way?

No. For most people who consider themselves bisexual, their feelings of sexual attraction are usually stronger for one gender than the other. For example, David is a nineteen-year-old college student who considers himself bisexual, but he's mostly attracted to men. "Right now I have a boyfriend, but I also really like women. I'm more sexually attracted to men, but there are certain women I find really attractive and I'm more comfortable with them emotionally. I don't know, but that's how I feel." Helen is also a college student and she also finds men more sexually attractive than women, but in the past she's been attracted to women, too, and had a girlfriend for a short time. "I think I'll probably wind up with a guy, but you never know. If I fall in love with a woman first, that could be it. But I'm not in any rush to settle down with anyone for a long time."

**I thought bisexuals were just gay people who were confused or afraid to admit they're gay. Is that true?**

Some people think that men and women who call themselves bisexual are really gay, but are just afraid to say it. While it's true that some gay men and women adopt the "bisexual" label as they're sorting out and learning to accept their true feelings, there are in fact some people who have feelings of sexual attraction for both men and women. These people are not confused, afraid, or pretending. They're simply bisexual.

**Do you have to have sex to know if you're gay or not?**

No, most people have a pretty good idea of what their feelings of sexual attraction are long before they have a sexual experience with anyone. You can know from just how you feel inside. But sometimes it does take a sexual and/or emotional experience for someone to understand and recognize what their true feelings are. For example, over the years I've interviewed many women who said they knew they felt different, but didn't realize what that difference was until they fell in love with another woman for the first time and/or had a sexual experience with a woman.

The men I've talked to, in general, had a clearer idea at an earlier age of what their feelings of attraction were, so a sexual experience only confirmed for them what they already knew to be true. For example, I remember kissing girls at summer camp and thinking it was nice, but nothing all that special, at least not as special as the other boys seemed to think it was. I didn't think of myself as gay at that age, although I knew I had crushes on some of my male counselors.

I still didn't want to think of myself as gay when I was seventeen and had a crush on Bob, a gay college student who lived down the street. Given how bad I thought it was to be gay, I was trying hard to ignore my feelings. But those feelings were very strong and when I finally kissed Bob, that was it. It felt like the most natural thing in the world for me and it was amazing. For the first time I really understood why the boys at camp would want to get up in the middle of the night and crawl through the woods in the hope of getting to kiss a girl. It's just that I felt that way about a guy, and after that first experience, there was no doubt in my mind that I was gay.

## Why can't you just pretend that you're not gay?

Plenty of people who are gay pretend that they're heterosexual, at least for a time. But it's not easy. In fact, it's just as difficult for someone who is gay to pretend to be heterosexual as it would be for someone who is heterosexual to pretend to be gay.

For example, just imagine for a few minutes that you live in a world where most people are gay. That's a fun thing to imagine for someone who is gay, but what if you're a heterosexual boy and you don't want anyone to know that you're different from most people? Well, you can never talk about the girls you're attracted to. You have to bring a male date to the junior prom. And when you get older, you'll be expected to marry a boy and have sex with him. So you see, pretending isn't so easy.

In years past, when gay and lesbian people faced far more prejudice and weren't nearly as accepted as they are now, most pretended they were heterosexual for their entire lives. Often that included getting married to someone of the other gender and having children. But as many people have discovered, pretending to be someone you're not can be incredibly difficult and can lead to great unhappiness.

**If you're sexually abused can that make you gay?**
No. Some people think that you can become gay if you are sexually abused or if you have a bad sexual experience with someone of the other gender. They are wrong. You may be angry, confused, or saddened by what has happened to you, but your feelings of sexual attraction—your sexual orientation—cannot be changed as a result of sexual abuse or a bad sexual experience.

**If I think I'm gay, lesbian, or bisexual, what should I do?**
It's a good idea to learn as much as you can and to find someone you can talk to who is knowledgeable and trustworthy. That's because it's important for you to understand yourself, and by finding someone to talk to, you won't feel alone. So the first thing you should do is read the rest of this book and see if you can find some of the other books I've listed in the "Resources" section. If you have access to the Internet, you should also have a look at some of the web sites I recommend, which provide all kinds of information, including where you may be able to find organizations for young people in your community. Some of the web sites also offer opportunities to meet

other young people who are gay, lesbian, or bisexual. (Please read my caution in the "Resources" section before using the Internet to research gay issues or to meet young people online.)

I know that many kids who think they're gay, lesbian, or bisexual are afraid they're all alone. But you're not alone. The challenge is finding someone you can talk to—someone you can trust and who will understand what you're feeling. That person may be a teacher, school counselor, friend, or relative. If you're lucky, there may be a GSA (gay-straight alliance) at your high school, a gay youth support group in your community, or a chapter of PFLAG (Parents, Families, and Friends of Lesbians and Gays) nearby. At all of these organizations, you'll find people who you can talk to who understand what you're going through. (See "Resources" for more information.)

### Is it true that being gay is like a disease?

No. Homosexuality is not a disease or sickness. However, at one time, people who were sexually attracted to those of the same gender were mistakenly considered mentally ill. But in the early 1970s, both the American Psychological Association and the American Psychiatric Association recognized their error and removed homosexuality from the list of mental illnesses. Nonetheless, there are still a small number of psychiatrists and psychologists who mistakenly believe that gay and lesbian people are by nature mentally ill and that they can be "cured." These people are considered by their peers to be far outside the mainstream of their professions and their work to "cure" homosexuality is not supported by our current understandings of human sexuality. These misguided psychiatrists and psychologists hold out false hope to those gay and lesbian people who are unhappy with being gay and are searching for a "cure." Homosexuality is not an illness, so there is nothing to be cured. However, because many gay and lesbian people grow up thinking they are "bad", it can be helpful to talk to an understanding mental health professional to get over those negative feelings.

### I've heard that being gay is "bad" or "nasty." Is that true?

No, this is not true. Homosexuality is not bad or nasty. But many people have been taught to believe this by their families, friends, and religious leaders. These beliefs are based on myths and mis-understandings about the nature of homosexuality and misunderstandings about the ways in which gay and lesbian people lead their lives. For example, one myth is that you become gay because you are brought up by a strong mother and a weak father.

### Some people say that being gay is unnatural? Are they right?

No. Being gay or lesbian is natural by definition, because it occurs in nature—and not just among humans. Scientists have studied all kinds of animals that engage in homosexual behavior, from mountain rams to seagulls to gorillas. Also, gay and lesbian people who are comfortable with their sexuality will tell you that their experience of having a sexual relationship with someone of the same gender feels perfectly natural to them, just as natural as it does for heterosexual people who have a sexual relationship with someone of the other gender.

### Is homosexuality abnormal?

No, homosexuality is normal. That's because something is normal if it's not unusual. Given how many gay and lesbian people there are, we know that it's not unusual.

Let's look at this another way. We don't consider left-handed people abnormal. They're simply different from the majority, most of whom happen to be right-handed. Years ago left-handed people were thought to be abnormal or defective, just as many people today still believe that gay men and women are abnormal. Like left-handedness, being gay is simply different from the majority and is absolutely normal.

### My minister says that homosexuality is immoral and sinful. What do you think?

I don't believe that homosexuality is immoral or sinful. But morality and religious beliefs are a matter of personal choice, something that each of us must decide on his or her own. (See chapter 5, "God and Religion," for more on this topic.)

### Do gay boys look at other boys in the locker room? Do lesbians look at other girls in the locker room?

Yes, and heterosexual boys look at other boys and heterosexual girls look at other girls. People are curious by nature, whether they're heterosexual or gay. So when it comes to the locker room, most boys look at other boys and most girls look at other girls. This is true whether you're in middle school, college, or at a neighborhood gym.

## Are there a lot of gay and lesbian people?

Yes, there are. But since a lot of gay and lesbian people remain hidden—they don't talk about it or they pretend that they're heterosexual—no one knows exactly how many gay men and women there are. From all I've read, I believe that about 5 percent of men and about 2 or 3 percent of women are gay. Other people believe the total is closer to 10 percent. But whatever the exact number, there are tens of millions of gay people around the world and the odds are that there are gay men and women in every extended family in America.

Also, in recent years, gay, lesbian, and bisexual people together have emerged as a powerful block of voters. In the 1996 presidential election, 5 percent of voters identified themselves as gay, lesbian, or bisexual. And as a percentage of the total electorate, openly gay, lesbian, and bisexual people are a larger group than Jewish and Asian-American people combined.

## Where do gay and lesbian people live?

Gay and lesbian people live in all parts of the country and in every community. But for a long time, many gay people have chosen to live in the nation's big cities—

including Chicago, Houston, New York, Los Angeles, San Francisco, San Diego, Seattle, Boston, Miami, and Atlanta—and they've done so for several reasons. Some gay people left their small towns and cities to get away from families and communities where they feared and/or experienced prejudice. Others chose to live in big cities because they wanted to be in places where there were many more chances to meet other gay people like themselves. And because of the large numbers of gay men and women living in the big cities, there are also many different kinds of gay and lesbian organizations for people to join, from sports clubs and political organizations, to gay and lesbian churches and synagogues.

In recent years, as prejudice has decreased and gay men and lesbians have felt more comfortable being themselves, more and more gay men and lesbians have felt less of a need to leave their home communities and cities to move to larger cities simply because of their sexual orientation.

### What kind of future can you have if you're lesbian or gay?

Jennifer, who grew up in Denver and now attends college in northern Colorado, told me, "I see myself living a happy life with a long-term relationship. I see living the same life as my sister, only she'll be married to a guy and I'll be married to a girl. I just don't know about the whole kid thing."

Jennifer, like most young gay and lesbian people, can look forward to a life much the same as any young person, despite remaining prejudice. But because of that prejudice, many parents worry that their gay and lesbian children may face more challenges than their heterosexual brothers and sisters.

When my mother first found out that I was gay, she told me that she was sad that I'd never have a happy relationship. I pointed out that from what I could tell, being heterosexual didn't seem to be any guarantee of having a happy relationship; she and my father separated when I was ten. But my mother's concern was genuine. At the time, 1977, she didn't know any gay or lesbian couples (and neither did I for that matter). She was also concerned that because of prejudice, I'd have fewer career opportunities and she was also afraid that people would look down on me. My mom asked if I had any idea how much more difficult my life would be, and I didn't really have an answer for her, because I didn't know. But I did know that no matter how hard it might be, hiding the fact I was gay or pretending to be heterosexual would be harder.

Today, we know that gay people have loving, long-lasting relationships; more and more gay and lesbian people are choosing to have children of their own; openly gay people hold jobs in just about any profession you can imagine (with the major exception of the United States military, which still actively discriminates against openly gay men and lesbians); and while many heterosexuals look down on gay people, with each passing year more and more are discovering that gay men and lesbians are pretty much like everyone else, especially in their hopes and dreams for the future.

### How can you tell if someone is gay or lesbian? Do they look or act a certain way?

Most of the time you can't tell if someone is gay or lesbian. But growing up, I thought that all gay men were feminine and that all lesbians were masculine, so I figured that you could always tell. It turns out that the truth is more complicated than that. While some gay men are feminine and some lesbians are masculine, most are no different in manner and appearance from the average heterosexual man or woman, so it's generally difficult to look at someone and be able to tell whether or not they're gay.

Something to think about: not all men who are feminine are gay and not all women who are masculine are lesbians. At the same time, not all men who are masculine and not all women who are feminine are heterosexual. As I said, the truth is complicated.

**If you are a gay boy, do you eventually have limp wrists and talk like you're gay? If you are a lesbian, do you become masculine and get very athletic?**

No. Most gay men who are feminine and most lesbians who are masculine were born that way. They are not trying to be feminine or masculine. They are just being themselves.

**Do gay men want to be women? Do lesbians want to be men?**

No. Gay men are happy being male and lesbians are happy being female. People who are not happy that they were born male or female, or in other words, "feel trapped in the body of the other gender," are called transgender. (For more information about transgender people, see "Resources.")

### Are transgender people gay?

Just like anyone else, transgender people can be heterosexual, homosexual, or bisexual. How people experience being male or female, masculine or feminine, has nothing to do with their feelings of sexual attraction for others.

### What does it mean when a gay person "comes out of the closet"?

It means to tell the truth about their sexual orientation—to themselves, to friends, to family, or to anyone who doesn't know that they're gay or lesbian.

In other words, when I "came out" to my friends, I told them I was gay. Before that, I was hiding the truth from them, as if I were hiding my true self in an imaginary closet. Then when I felt comfortable about being gay and trusted that my friends would still love me if they knew the truth, I "came out of the closet."

### What does "outing" mean?

Let's say that you're gay and you don't want anyone to know about it, except maybe your closest friends and family. Then someone who knows that you're gay decides to tell everyone the truth about your sexual orientation. That's "outing" someone. In other words, "outing" means revealing the truth about a gay person's sexual orientation against their wishes. For example, sometimes celebrities have been "outed" in magazines or on television. In general, I've always believed that it's up to the individual person to decide whether to come out or stay in the closet.

**Why do some people think that gay men and lesbians should keep their sexual orientation a secret?**
People believe this for a variety of reasons. Some think that being gay is so wrong and sinful that gay men and women should be embarrassed to reveal the truth. Some think that an openly gay relative will reflect badly on family members if other people know about it. Others think that if gay people are public about their sexual orientation, they'll somehow be a bad influence on children. Still others are concerned that if someone they care about is openly gay, he or she may be subject to prejudice and mistreatment. And some people haven't really thought about why, but they just wish gay people would go back in the closet, in other words, go back to being "invisible" the way they were in past generations.

When I first told my grandmother I was gay, she had a difficult time understanding why I couldn't just keep it a secret. She said, "I understand that this is how it is and that you're not going to change, but why do you have to tell anyone?" My grandmother didn't understand that it's not like keeping a secret about an upcoming surprise birthday party.

Because your sexual orientation involves many aspects of your life, especially when you get older and begin having relationships, you often wind up having to answer questions with lies if you want to keep it a secret. People ask questions all the time, like "Do you have a boyfriend?" "Do you have a girlfriend?" "Are you married?" "Are the two of you brothers?" So keeping your sexual orientation a secret becomes a huge job, because you can never say anything that might reveal the truth, even if you have to lie and make up stories. And that can make a person feel very alone, as if nobody knows who they really are.

We don't ask heterosexual people to keep their feelings secret, because we think that the love between a man and a woman is a great thing. So there's no good reason for them to hide something that is such a natural part of themselves. I think the same should be true for gay people. Loving another person is a perfectly natural thing for gay men and women, so why should they have to hide it?

**Why do some gay people keep their sexual orientation a secret or pretend that they're heterosexual?**
There are many reasons: They don't want to risk getting teased or beaten up at school; they don't want to risk being rejected by their friends and families; they feel bad or embarrassed about being gay; they want to "fit in"; they have conservative anti-gay religious beliefs; they don't want people to look down on them; and they want to avoid being discriminated against at work.

Jackson, the seventeen-year-old high school student who has been attracted to guys since kindergarten, is afraid that if his friends and family know the truth, they'll look down on him. To make sure they don't find out, he's dating a girl at school. "Having a girlfriend means they won't think I'm gay. It's tough because my girlfriend expects me to have sex with her, but I can't imagine doing it."

Mae is eighteen and lives in a small town about an hour from Atlanta, Georgia. While she's told all of her classmates and her mother that she's gay, she hasn't brought up the subject with her father or stepmother because she's afraid of how they'll react. "My step-mom is really religious and my dad has become that way. I'm putting it off for now. But I'll probably tell them in the near future. I've been debating about how to tell him."

When Mark was growing up on eastern Long Island, he thought he would have to keep his sexual orientation a secret forever because of what he heard at his Pentecostal church. "I remember sitting in church feeling very nervous, because every other week, from out of nowhere, the pastor would list the sins of the world: abortion, homosexuality, and Democrats. To be honest, I thought I was going to hell. I thought everyone would hate me if they ever found out."

### Who are some famous living gay people who haven't kept it a secret?

My short list includes retired tennis great Martina Navratilova; four-time Olympic gold medalist diving champion Greg Louganis; the 1996 U.S. figure-skating champion Rudy Galindo; actors Amanda Bearse (*Married with Children*), Wilson Cruz (*My So-Called Life*), Ellen DeGeneres, Rupert Everett, Anne Heche, and Sir Ian McKellen; Massachusetts Congressman Barney Frank; business moguls Barry Diller and David Geffen; and singers Melissa Etheridge, Elton John, k.d. lang, George Michael,

Sinead O'Connor, and the Indigo Girls; and Chastity
Bono and Ru Paul.

**Why do some kids call other kids "fag" or "faggot" or
say things like, "Don't be so gay," or "That's so gay."**
A lot of kids don't know exactly what the words
"faggot" or "gay" mean, but they use them as curse
words and put-downs. They know when they call
someone a "faggot" or say, "That's so gay," that
what they're saying is "You're something nasty; you're
something bad; you're clueless; that's dumb; that's
boring; that's disgusting."

The word "faggot" has long been a slur word used
against men and boys who were thought to be weak,
bookish, and sensitive. They weren't necessarily gay,
but they weren't masculine in the way many people
think men should be. People also used the words
"lesbian" and "dyke" to put down women who were
athletic, who took leadership roles, or who weren't
feminine in the way some people think women
should be, regardless of their sexual orientation.

Today, "fag" and "faggot" are still used as a slur
against gay men, as well as men and boys who are
simply not considered masculine, regardless of their
sexual orientation. "Fag" is also used more generally

as a slur word, as in "Stop joking around. You're being such a fag."

The word "gay" was adopted in the late 1960s and early 1970s by a new generation of gay rights activists, who preferred it over the more clinical sounding "homosexual" or "homophile." It wasn't until recent years that the word "gay" has come to be used as a slur or curse among young people.

## What does "queer" mean? Is it a slur?

When I was growing up, you called a kid a "queer" if you thought he was gay; "queer" was used as a slur word, like "fag." Some gay people also used "queer" in a playful way among themselves.

In the 1990s, a new generation of young gay people started using "queer" as a substitute for "gay" or "lesbian." They didn't see "queer" as a slur word anymore, but instead embraced it as an inclusive word that took in all kinds of people, including gay men, lesbians, bisexuals, transgender people, and anyone else who was considered outside the mainstream. The word also came to be used in academic programs, as in "Queer Studies." Despite the new use of "queer," there are many gay people who still find the word offensive.

**What is it like when people care about someone gay—like a friend or uncle or parent—and they hear anti-gay language?**

For people who know and care about a person who is gay, hearing someone use anti-gay slurs can make them feel uncomfortable, upset, angry, frightened, or hurt. And it also puts them in the often difficult position of trying to figure out what, if anything, to say in response.

Erica is in the sixth grade at a private school in Maryland and she has an uncle who is gay. Every day at school she hears kids call each other "faggot" and use put-downs like "That's so gay." She told me, "It makes me really, really uncomfortable, and I'll give them that look that says, 'Stop it. It's not nice to make fun of these people.' But I'm afraid to say something direct. It makes me scared. A lot of times it's hard to stand up for what you think, because you feel outnumbered."

Chris Lord, one of Erica's teachers, has made no secret of the fact that his father is gay and that he has no patience for anti-gay language. "My father and mother split when I was very young and I didn't meet my father until five years ago, which is when I first found out he was gay. But it wasn't an issue for me.

My mom always had gay friends. When I was very young, I didn't really understand what it meant to be gay, but it became something natural to me. So from an early age I had a problem with those words. It still makes me cringe when I hear them."

**What's it like for someone who is gay or lesbian when they hear someone use the word "fag" or hear someone say, "That's so gay"?**
It feels bad when you hear people say these things, especially if you hear it from friends or family. But it can also make you angry. And if the words are meant for you, it can feel very threatening and scary.

Mae was in ninth grade when her classmates started calling her names. "It was just a rumor that I was gay. My girlfriend and I had just broken up. She wanted to get back at me, so she told everyone I was gay. Just walking down the hall, people called me a dyke and a lesbo. These were people who had been my friends and decided not to be anymore, and people I didn't even know, but they'd heard I was gay. It hurt. And it made me angry. Anyone calling you a name is going to make you angry."

Kevin, who is gay and attends high school in southern California, is the president of his school's

GSA (gay-straight alliance). He's very open about being gay and is routinely called names by a handful of students. "Under their breath they'll say, 'faggot.' They never do it in an obvious way, because at my high school if someone yelled out 'faggot' at another student, they'd be shunned." Kevin says that he doesn't let it bother him because he knows he'll have a good life no matter what these students say.

Besides the under-the-breath name-calling, Kevin said that kids at his school also routinely say "fag" and "gay" as slur words, but it's not directed at anyone in particular and he doesn't let that bother him either. "I take it with a grain of salt because most of them don't know what they're saying. Most kids are pretty smart and if they knew that what they were saying was hurting people, they wouldn't say it."

I wish I could agree with Kevin, but I think a lot of kids know what they're saying, or at least they know that using these words will be hurtful. For example, I remember being at summer camp when I was fourteen and a girl I didn't want to date decided to get back at me by telling my cabin-mates that I was a "fag." From then on, my cabin-mates, as well as some of the other kids at camp, called me "faggot." They intended to hurt me with that word and they succeeded.

As an adult, because of my work, I've been called "faggot" every now and then. It still makes me cringe—it's a reflex—but that kind of language doesn't hurt me as it did when I was young. Mostly, now, it just makes me sad, because I'd hoped that by now people would know better. Unfortunately, prejudice in all its ugly forms is still alive and well here in the United States and around the world.

**If you hear someone using anti-gay language or someone calls you "faggot" or "dyke," should you say something?**
For kids, I have only one rule when it comes to saying something in response to people who use the word "gay" as a slur or use other anti-gay language: You should never say anything if you think that saying it could put you in some sort of danger. Also, if you are gay, by challenging someone's remarks you might bring unwanted attention to yourself, especially if you don't want anyone to know that you're gay.

Of course, each situation is different and even if there doesn't seem to be any danger in challenging someone, it can be very scary to stand up on your own and say what you think. (Even at my age, I still find it difficult to challenge people who make negative remarks about gay people.) But if you find yourself in a position to say something, you can simply respond by saying, "I don't like hearing those words, I find them offensive, and they're hurtful to people who are gay and lesbian."

When it comes to teachers and parents, I think it's absolutely their responsibility to make clear that anti-gay language is wrong and that it shouldn't be used by anyone at any time. Unfortunately, teachers and parents can sometimes be prejudiced or afraid, or they simply might not know what to say. (For more on why teachers might be afraid, see chapter 6, "School.")

I wish all parents and teachers could be as confident and clear as one of my old friends. When she recently heard her nine-year-old son call his younger brother a "faggot," she knew he didn't understand exactly what he had said. So she sat him down and offered this simple, but firm explanation: "I said that 'faggot' was a mean word for someone who was gay, and that 'gay' was a word used to describe two people of the same sex who love each other in the same way that his dad and I love each other. I told him that some people love someone of the same sex, instead of the opposite sex, and that I had some friends who were gay. I told him that these words hurt their feelings a lot, and I didn't use these words and didn't like them. I said that I love my friends and I didn't want them to be hurt. I also said that 'gay' wasn't a bad word but people sometimes used it in a mean way. My son doesn't like to hurt anyone's feelings, so I think he understood."

# chapter 2

# Friends and Family

**If I think my friend is gay, can I ask him/her about it?
What should I say?**

Yes, you can ask your friend. But before you do, keep in mind that if your friend is gay, he or she may be afraid to answer honestly, especially if your friend is unsure how you feel about gay people. If your friend has been keeping his or her sexual orientation a secret, he or she might also be afraid that you won't keep the secret. So, you need to make sure your friend knows that you are asking out of concern and that you can be trusted. For example, you can say, "You're my friend. I care about you and really want to understand you. I've been wondering if you might be gay. I want you to know that if you are, I'm okay with that and you can trust me not to tell anyone if you don't want me to."

Depending on his or her circumstances, your friend could respond in a number of different ways. If, for example, she says yes, that she's gay, then that can be the beginning of a much longer conversation and a better friendship. If she isn't gay, she'll tell you she's not. And because some people think that being gay is a bad thing, she might also be upset that you would think she was. If she doesn't yet have a full understanding of her feelings, she might say that she isn't gay or that she's unsure. And even if she is gay and knows it, she may still not be comfortable telling you. That's what happened with Mae and her best friend.

In ninth grade, when Mae's best friend asked her if she was gay, she said that she wasn't, that the rumors at school were just rumors. Mae told me, "I was scared of her reaction. She said it didn't matter either way, but regardless of what she said, I was still afraid that it might change something. Me and her were good friends and I didn't want that to change." But Mae did take comfort in thinking that her friend was someone she might be able to talk to one day.

## How do you get up the courage to ask?

First you need to think about why you're scared. Are you afraid that your friend will be mad if you ask? Are you afraid that you could be wrong? Are you afraid that you'll hurt your friendship if you're wrong?

In the worst case, which isn't really so bad, you could be wrong and your friend might get mad. But if you're right, then by asking, you've given your friend an opportunity to talk about what he or she is feeling and that will make you better friends. A lot of times, gay people are afraid of how their friends will react if they tell the truth, so they hesitate to say anything unless someone asks them.

It's perfectly normal to be afraid of the unknown. That's a good reason to be careful and to think about what to say, but that's not a good reason to give up on trying to be a good friend.

## I think my best friend is gay/lesbian. Will he or she want to have sex with me?

One of the myths about gay people is that they're

sexually attracted to everyone of the same gender. This is just a myth. Gay people are like heterosexual people in that they're sexually attracted only to some people, not to most. You probably don't worry about your heterosexual friends wanting to have sex with you, and just the same, there is no reason to worry that your gay friends will want to have sex with you. And in any case, if a friend wants to have sex with you and you don't want to, all you have to do is tell him or her that you're not interested.

**I have a friend who is gay and very upset about it. My friend has talked about committing suicide. What should I do?**

You should take what your friend says as seriously as you would any friend who talks about committing suicide. The first thing to do is encourage your friend to talk to an adult. If your friend can't or won't do that, then you need to get immediate help for your friend. This is not something you can be responsible for on your own and you must talk to an adult—a teacher, school counselor or nurse, or a parent—and tell them that you have a friend who has talked about committing suicide. If your friend has confided in you that he or she is gay, you can still get help for your friend without telling anyone the reason for your friend's wish to commit suicide. If you don't feel comfortable talking to any of the adults you know, call a local suicide crisis telephone hotline (look in your phone book or call information) or you can call the national teen crisis hotline listed in the "Resources" section.

### I'm gay and I'd like to tell my friends, but I'm afraid to. What should I do?

It's perfectly natural to want to tell your friends that you're gay. Not telling them means keeping a big secret about yourself and maybe even having to pretend that you're not gay. It's also perfectly natural to be afraid of saying anything. Some people have bad feelings about homosexuality, so it's scary to bring up the subject with people who are important to you, especially if you don't know how they might react. Will they still want to be your friend? Will they look down on you? Will they be supportive? Will they be scared?

Jennifer, who is gay and is now in her second year of college, told all of her friends after she graduated from high school. But, she said, "You should be cautious about the people you tell. Before I told everyone I was gay, I said to them, 'How judgmental are you?' And if they said, 'Not very,' I then asked, 'Will you love me no matter what?' And if they said, 'Yes,' then I told them I was gay. I've never had one person say I can't be your friend because of it."

Kevin, who is open about being gay at his southern California high school, suggested that you think about your friends' attitudes before telling them that you're gay. He said, "Test the waters. Kids will generally know if their friends are accepting."

You can also test your friends by bringing up the subject. You can talk about something you saw on television, or if you have a gay relative, you can talk about him or her. If your friend responds with very strong negative feelings, then your friend will probably have difficulty with the news that you're gay. If, however, your friend is open and supportive of gay people or just neutral, then you know that this is a friend you can probably talk to.

Mae, who is now a high school senior, has told all of her friends that she's gay and most of her classmates at school know as well. She offered this final note of caution: "When you come out, there's always going to be somebody who doesn't agree with it or somebody who hurts your feelings. So you have to be strong enough to handle that. And I know that not everybody can." If you don't think you're strong enough yet, then the best thing to do is wait until you feel that you are. You'll know when that is.

### How do people react when they find out a friend is gay?

Good friends should be supportive and understanding, which is how fourteen-year-old Tony's friends reacted when he first talked to them. He wrote to me, "My friends were all really cool when I told 'em I was gay, but they already knew. Now we talk about guys and stuff all the time. (Oh, yeah, all of my friends were straight girls at the time.)"

But not everyone is instantly supportive and understanding. If people are prejudiced or have traditional religious beliefs, they may not want to be friends once they discover that a friend is gay. That's what happened to Mae when she was in the ninth grade. Her friends heard rumors that she was gay and most of them avoided her. She recalled, "People who I thought were my friends didn't want to have anything to do with me, just because of that."

Two of Mae's friends, Misty and Kendall, stuck by her. But because she was afraid of how they might react, she told them that the rumors weren't true. A year later, when Mae told Misty that she really was gay, Misty got mad. "She was mad because I didn't come out and tell her the truth in the first place. She told me that she thought we were better friends than that. I didn't trust that she was telling the truth, but I should have. After she got over being mad, everything was fine."

Friends can also react with surprise or confusion, especially if they never considered the possibility that their friend could be gay. But more often than not, good friends do their best to be understanding and may even be very curious about what it's like to be gay. Caroline, who is sixteen and plays on her high school's tennis team in south Florida, has confided in only a couple of her friends after they asked her directly if she was gay. She said, "At first I tried to give the impression that I wasn't, because I was so scared they would hate me. But then I started crying and told them the truth. They were my friends. I couldn't lie to them. And it turned out that they were great. They didn't think it was any big deal. Now they think I'm some sort of expert and they ask me questions all the time."

## I have a crush on my friend. Can I tell him/her?

Maybe. But before you say anything, you have to think about this carefully. First, whether you're gay or heterosexual, there is always the risk that your friend will not have the same feelings for you, so you have to be prepared for that possibility.

Second, if you happen to be gay or lesbian, there are a few other risks to consider depending upon your situation. For example, I recently received an e-mail from Steven, who attends a middle school in a small southern city. He wrote, "I have a new friend who moved here a few months ago. I like him a lot and we spend a lot of time together and I think I have a crush on him. I don't think he knows I'm gay and I don't know if he's gay. I want to tell him how I feel, but I'm afraid he won't feel the same way."

As I learned from later e-mails, Steven has not yet told his parents that he's gay and has not told anyone at school either. He doesn't plan to tell his parents until he's older because they're very traditional. He also thinks it would be a really bad idea for anyone at school to find out he's gay. He also doesn't know his friend's attitudes towards gay people, although he's never heard him say anything negative.

So here are the risks if Steven decides to tell his

friend about his crush on him. In the worst case, the friend could reject him and then decide to tell other kids at school that Steven is gay. The friend might also tell his parents that Steven is gay, and they might then contact Steven's parents.

I suggested to Steven that given his situation, it was not a good idea to share his feelings with his friend. But I also suggested that he could find out more about his friend's attitudes towards gay people, and if his friend turned out to be supportive and was trustworthy, then he might decide to tell his friend that he's gay. And if it turned out that his friend was also gay and could be trusted, then Steven could consider telling his friend about his crush.

When you get older and you no longer live at home and don't have to worry about how your classmates would react if they knew you were gay, it's far less risky to tell someone you have a crush on him or her. But even when you're an adult, you still face the risk that the person you have a crush on won't feel the same way about you.

**My friend who is gay told me she/he has a crush on me. What should I say?**

If you like your friend in the same way, then you can tell your friend how you feel. If you don't feel the same as your friend does, then tell her or him that you're sorry, but you don't have the same feelings. It may feel awkward to be that direct, but that's often the best way.

**I'm not gay, but I like hanging out with my gay friends. Is there something wrong with me?**

There is absolutely nothing wrong with you. Many heterosexual people have gay friends. And many gay people have heterosexual friends.

**Can I ask my gay friends questions about what it's like to be gay?**

Yes, you can ask, and as long as your questions are respectful and show a real desire to understand, most gay and lesbian people will be happy to answer them. But keep in mind that not every gay person is comfortable talking about being gay or has the answers to your specific questions. In addition, your friend can only speak for him- or herself. Like heterosexuals, gay people have a variety of experiences and opinions. So it's also a good idea to do a little independent research of your own, like reading this book and other books or checking out some of the web sites I recommend.

I've been surprised by how rarely my heterosexual friends have asked me questions about being gay. I've written several books about gay people, so they know I'm not shy about the subject. Finally, I asked some of my friends why they haven't asked me questions. Most told me that they were afraid to say something that might hurt my feelings and they didn't want me to think they were stupid. (I've always believed that the only stupid question is the one you don't ask.)

Some gay people don't like answering questions because they feel heterosexuals should already know about gay people and how they live. But I think gay women and men have an obligation to help heterosexuals understand what gay people are like and how lesbians and gay men live their lives. If gay people don't help educate heterosexuals, who will?

### I'm gay. How can I become friends with other kids who are gay and lesbian?

The first challenge is finding other gay and lesbian people who are your age. For people who are college-aged or older, there are many opportunities to meet other gay people and to make friends (depending, of course, on where you go to school or where you live). It's much more difficult if you're in middle school or high school, because most kids that age are still coming to an understanding of their sexuality. And even kids who already understand that they're gay generally keep it a secret until after high school.

If you attend a school that has a GSA (gay-straight alliance) or if there is a gay and lesbian youth group in your community, then you will likely be able to make friends with other gay kids. One girl wrote to me about how she travels by bus from her small town to a nearby city to attend a weekly gay youth support group. Her parents think she's volunteering at a center for senior citizens and so far haven't discovered that she's spending every Sunday afternoon talking with other teens who are gay. "I know I'm taking a chance, but it's a risk I have to take. There's no one at my school I can talk to and my parents are very religious, so I can't talk to them."

If, like most young people, you don't attend a school that has a GSA and you don't live in a place where there is a gay youth group, another way to make friends is through the Internet. Always remember that when meeting people online, you should use the same caution you would when meeting any stranger. (See "Resources" for further caution on using the Internet and for more information.)

### How do parents react when they find out a child is lesbian or gay?

Parents react in all kinds of ways. Some are immediately understanding and loving while others react with confusion, sadness, tears, denial, guilt, embarrassment, anger, or hostility. Some parents even reject their children, going so far as to throw them out of the house. While this is the exception, it happens.

More typically, parents may wonder what they did wrong, they may express concern about AIDS, they may be upset that a child has not talked to them sooner, and they may hope that this is just a phase, especially if their child is still a youngster. All too often their reactions are based on the myths and stereotypes that they grew up with and not on the truth about what it means to be gay or lesbian.

For parents who have strong traditional or fundamentalist religious beliefs, the discovery that a child is gay or lesbian can be especially difficult. These parents will likely find themselves torn between what their religion tells them about homosexuality and their love for their children. (Please see chapter 5, "God and Religion," for more on this topic.)

My own mother's reaction was pretty average. She didn't cry or feel guilty, but she was disappointed, sad, worried, and confused, which left me feeling pretty awful. No one likes to disappoint his mother. She also didn't want me to tell anyone, because she was afraid of what people would think. In remembering the experience, she said, "I felt that if anyone knew, then my son would be stigmatized, rejected, looked at as defective or inferior. Somehow I couldn't bear the thought of someone judging him."

Like most parents, my mother eventually got used to my being gay. That was years ago, and now she's active in an organization called Parents, Families and Friends of Lesbians and Gays (PFLAG).

These days, because people know a lot more about homosexuality and have friends and family members who are openly gay, there are more and more parents who have thought about the possibility of a child being gay and are prepared if the subject comes up.

That was the case with nineteen-year-old Jennifer, who came out to her mother just a few months ago.

Jennifer recalled, "My mother was fine. She said she had known since I was twelve. One of her friends told her he thought I was gay. Looking back, I can remember my mother saying things like she knew. With my sister, she would say, "When you bring your husband home." With me, she would always say, "When you bring a person home."

Another example is a father I spoke with recently whose twelve-year-old daughter said that she thought she might be gay. "She asked me what I thought," he said. "I told her that I didn't know if she was gay, but that she would come to understand this about herself as she got older. I told her that it was not something she needed to worry about and that her mother and I would always love her. I also told her that when she fell in love that we would love that person, too, whether that person was a girl or a boy." The world would be a much better place if all parents responded with this kind of love and understanding.

**If I think I'm gay, can I tell my parents?**
Maybe. But before you do anything, you need to think carefully about how your parents are likely to react. That's because not all parents are loving and supportive of their gay children. Some parents can

react very badly to the news that a child is gay. Some have even completely rejected their gay children and forced them to leave home. Others have sent their children away to special programs that are designed to "turn" gay kids into heterosexuals. While these cases are generally the exception, you still need to get a very good idea of how your parents will react before you say anything.

If there is any reason for you to think that your parents will react badly, then the best thing to do is to find other people to talk to now and to wait until you're older and no longer living at home or financially dependent on your parents before you tell them that you're gay or lesbian.

## How can I figure out how my parents will react if I tell them I'm gay?

You can never be absolutely certain how a parent will react, but you can get a pretty good idea of whether your parents will react with understanding and concern or with anger and hostility. If your parents are the kind of people you talk to about everything, and they have talked positively about gay issues and gay people in the past, then you can expect your parents will come to accept what you tell them. If, however, your parents hold fundamentalist religious beliefs or have expressed negative opinions about gay people, you can expect that they will have a very difficult time and may never come to terms with what you tell them.

Kevin, who is in high school and lives with his mother, has what I think is a good plan of action for trying to figure out what your parents think and how they might react. He told me, "If you don't know what your parents think, you need to find out before you tell them you're gay. You need to scope them out. Let's say you're watching TV with your mom and dad, and there's a gay interest story or news story. Ask them what they think. Or just bring up that you have a gay friend and maybe talk about how he's having a problem with his parents and what do they think of that."

When it came to talking to his own mother, Kevin said, "I just knew she was neutral about it. But then we're not highly religious people. The last time my mom and I went to church together was probably five years ago. That was the first clue I had that she didn't have an opinion either way. So when I told her, she cried for three days, and then said, 'I don't want grandchildren anyway.' So I told my mother that I wanted children. She rolled her eyes.

"If you come out, give your parents time and eventually they'll come around to it. In my case it was three days; in someone else's it might be thirty years."

**If I think I'm gay, but I can't talk to my parents, are there other parents I can talk to?**
Yes, absolutely. There are many thousands of parents across the country who are members of an organization called Parents, Families and Friends of Lesbians and Gays (PFLAG). Most members are parents who have gay and lesbian children themselves. If you contact your local chapter, you'll find an accepting mom or dad who has lots of experience with these issues. They will be more than happy to talk to you in confidence. And they will be happy to talk to your parents as well, if you wish. (Please see "Resources" for contact information.)

**If one of my close relatives, like my sister, father, or uncle, is gay, does that mean I'll be gay, too?**
No. Even if a close relative is gay, the odds are that you will be heterosexual.

**Will my gay relatives try to make me gay?**
No. Your gay relatives will not try to make you gay.

No one can make you gay, just as no one can make you heterosexual.

**My Aunt Sharon and Aunt Sonya are a lesbian couple, but I've never seen them touch each other or hold hands. Why not?**
This reminds me of a question my mother asked me nearly twenty years ago. She was concerned that my then boyfriend and I seemed so distant. She said, "You're never affectionate. Is there some sort of problem between the two of you?" Her question surprised me because my boyfriend and I were always physically affectionate, but I realized that she had no way of knowing. That's because we were affectionate only when we were alone or around other gay people, who we knew would be perfectly comfortable with us. We had grown up in a time when gay people generally avoided drawing attention to themselves by being physically affectionate. No one likes to be judged, stared at, called names, or physically attacked. I explained this to my mother and she said that she hoped we would feel comfortable enough to be ourselves when we were with her.

While times have changed in recent years, and gay people are more open than they were in the past, gay and lesbian couples are still often reluctant to be themselves in public situations, including family events like weddings.

Five years ago, when my cousin Rob got married, my partner, Barney, and I were the only gay couple among the three hundred guests. My cousin Bernice, who was also a guest at the wedding, very kindly came over to us and told us that she hoped we felt comfortable enough to dance just like everybody else. We thanked my cousin for her encouragement, but while I love to dance, Barney and I never danced together that night. I'm sure no one would have said anything, but knowing that we would have been the first same-gender couple to ever dance together at a Marcus family event, we just didn't feel comfortable drawing that much attention to ourselves.

The day after the family wedding, we attended the small wedding of my best friend and his bride. Barney and I felt completely comfortable in that setting, which included several other gay and lesbian people, so the two of us rarely left the dance floor. No one stared at us. No one commented. We all just had a great time. And it felt wonderful to be ourselves.

**My parents are divorced and I think it may be because one of them is gay. Is it okay to ask?**

You can ask, but that doesn't mean your parents will give you a direct answer. If, in fact, your mother or father is gay, your parents themselves may be having difficulty dealing with the situation and may not want to talk about it. They may also consider it a private matter between the two of them. They may think that you are too young to discuss it. Your gay parent may fear being rejected by you. Or your parents may fear that by talking with you about it that it will upset you or be a burden to you.

Some parents, however, are relieved to be asked. I remember one divorced friend whose sons asked one day over breakfast, "Mom, are you gay?" My friend was startled at first, because she didn't think her eight- and ten-year-old sons had any idea. "You can fool yourself into thinking that your kids don't know what's going on, but they knew and they were looking for confirmation. I thought it was only fair to tell them the truth." My friend had been afraid to tell her sons because she was scared of how they might react, but as she explained to me, "They didn't really care. They just wanted to be sure that I loved them. And, of course, I do. I'm so glad the whole thing is out in the open now and it's a non-issue."

**I live with my two moms. Why won't some of my friends' parents let my friends come to my house?**

Some people are still very uninformed about gay men and lesbians and they think that if their kids get to know gay men and women that it will somehow make their children gay. Other people mistakenly believe that gay men and women are more likely to molest their children. And still others think that being gay is wrong or sinful and don't want their children exposed to sinful people.

**I have a gay parent and I'd like to talk to other kids who are in the same boat. How do I find them?**

There is an organization for kids who have gay parents. It's called Children of Lesbians and Gays Everywhere (COLAGE). (See "Resources" for contact information.)

# chapter 3

# Dating,
# Getting Married, Kids

**Are gay men attracted to all men?**
**Are lesbians attracted to all women?**

**N**o, but some people believe that gay men are
attracted to every man, teenager, and boy they see.
And they imagine that lesbians are attracted to every
woman, teenager, and girl they see. That is just as
foolish as believing that heterosexual men and
women are attracted to every person of the other
gender. Sexual feelings of attraction are complex and
selective, which means you will be attracted to some

people, but not to most. And even if someone is attracted, that doesn't mean they'll act on their feelings.

**What do gay people do on a date?**
When gay people go on dates, they do the same things that heterosexuals do—except you're not as likely to see male couples and female couples holding hands or kissing in public.

**Why don't gay people hold hands and kiss in public?**
If there were no prejudice and gay and lesbian people were safe from discrimination, harassment, and worse, you would see gay and lesbian couples on dates holding hands or kissing in public just like some heterosexuals do. But that's not the case, so the places where you're most likely to see gay and lesbian couples being affectionate in public are those places where gay people feel safe. This includes places where there are large numbers of gay men and women, like neighborhoods where many gay and lesbian people live; popular gay and lesbian resorts, like Provincetown, Massachusetts; gay clubs and restaurants; and at public events, like gay pride parades and festivals.

**If two people of the same gender go on a date, who asks whom out on the date? Who pays?**

Traditionally, for heterosexuals, boys ask girls out and boys are expected to pay the expenses. This is no longer the strict rule that it was when my parents and grandparents were dating, but many heterosexual people still fall back on that tradition. For gay and lesbian people, that's not a tradition they can depend on for obvious reasons. But if the date is going to happen, someone has to do the asking. And the expenses still need to be paid, whether there are two women or two men on the date.

Without clearly defined roles based on who is the "boy" and who is the "girl," gay and lesbian people are relatively free to do what they want. So the person who does the asking is usually the one who feels more strongly about wanting to go on the date, is more comfortable doing the asking, or is less afraid of being rejected. And when it comes to who pays, there are also choices. The person who did the asking may want to pay, the two men or women may choose to pay their own way, the person who earns more money might want to pay, or the person who is more comfortable spending money may want to buy the movie tickets or pick up the dinner check.

### If a gay guy or a lesbian asks me out, what should I do?

Before you say anything, put yourself in the other person's shoes and imagine what it was like for him or her to get up the courage to ask you out in the first place. With this in mind, whatever you say, remember to be kind. If you're not interested, you can simply say, "Thank you, but I'm not interested." If you are interested, then this is your lucky day.

Sometimes heterosexual people react strongly when someone mistakenly assumes that they are gay. They get upset that anyone could think that they are gay, because they consider being gay something bad. But since being gay isn't bad, there is no reason to feel insulted or to get upset. If someone who is gay asks you out on a date, think of it as a compliment.

### Do gay people fall in love?

Just like everyone else, gay and lesbian people fall in love.

**When gay people have a relationship, is one the husband and one the wife? Is it different from how my parents are?**

Gay and lesbian people have couple relationships that are as varied as the couple relationships heterosexual people have. Some are like traditional heterosexual marriages, where one partner goes to work and the other stays home. But most gay and lesbian couples are like most heterosexual couples: both partners work, both contribute in different ways to taking care of the various household chores and responsibilities, and both share in decision-making.

**Can gay people get married?**

No. At this time, gay and lesbian people cannot get legally married in the United States. In other words, two men or two women cannot get a marriage license in any of the fifty states or the District of Columbia. However, the state of Vermont offers gay and lesbian couples the same benefits and responsibilities as heterosexual married couples. But instead of being called marriage, it's called a "civil union."

So if two men or two women want a "civil union" in the state of Vermont, they will have to apply for a "civil union" license from the town clerk, just as a heterosexual couple would apply for a marriage license. And once the gay spouses have been given the certificate, the law considers their roles to be just like those of heterosexual spouses when it comes to about two dozen different areas, including child custody law, probate law (the laws that govern inheritance), workers' compensation, and family leave benefits. Unfortunately, states outside Vermont and the federal government are not expected to recognize the legal status of Vermont's civil unions.

Also, in several European countries, including Sweden, Denmark, Norway, Spain, Iceland, Belgium, and the Netherlands, gay and lesbian couples can get legal protections that come close to or are the same as the legal protections given to married heterosexual couples. And Brazil gives gay and lesbian couples the right to inherit each other's pension and social security benefits. (In mid-2000, the government of Canada erased most legal differences between heterosexual and homosexual couples.)

**My two moms had a commitment ceremony. Is that the same thing as getting legally married?**
No. Any two people can have a religious or secular ceremony celebrating their love and commitment for

one another. But unless you have a marriage license and the ceremony is performed by someone who is authorized to conduct a legal wedding, then it is not a legally recognized marriage. No state currently gives a marriage license to gay and lesbian couples (although Vermont offers a "civil union" license to same-gender couples), but that hasn't stopped plenty of gay and lesbian couples from having commitment ceremonies of one kind or another.

For example, in June 1996, Barney and I had a commitment ceremony in the garden of a church across the street from our house. We had about two hundred guests, including our parents, my grandmother, our brothers and sisters, nieces and nephews, uncles and aunts, cousins, friends, neighbors, and colleagues. We had a friend conduct the ceremony (a sort of master of ceremonies), we exchanged vows and rings, and afterwards we had a big party at our house to celebrate. To us it was like a wedding, and in fact, whenever my grandmother talks about it, she calls it our wedding. And while we feel just as committed to each other as two married people, and love each other just as much as two married people, we can't get a marriage license, so we're not protected by the laws that protect heterosexual couples who get married.

Now that Vermont has passed its "civil union" law for gay and lesbian couples, Barney and I and many of our gay and lesbian couple friends plan to go to Vermont to get a "civil union" license. But because we live in New York, which won't recognize the Vermont license, our civil union will only be symbolic.

### If you feel married, why do you need a marriage license?

Gay and lesbian couples want to take care of each other (and their children if they have any) in the same way that heterosexual married couples do. And to do that, you need the legal rights that heterosexual people get when they are legally married.

When a man and a woman get legally married, they are automatically given the legal right to make medical decisions for one another in an emergency. They are automatically allowed to visit one another in a hospital intensive care unit. If one partner dies, the other automatically inherits the other's property and pension. If they choose to adopt a baby together, both automatically become the child's parents. And that's just a very short list of the kinds of legal rights and privileges that come with a marriage license. Gay and lesbian couples can approximate some of these things by drawing up special legal documents, but the documents only cover some things and are not recognized in all states.

Imagine for a minute what it would be like if your mother was ill and the hospital wouldn't let your dad visit or wouldn't listen to his decisions about her medical treatment. Is there any question that this would be wrong and unfair? Unfortunately, this sort of thing can and does happen to gay and lesbian couples.

### Why are people against gay and lesbian couples getting married?

Some people think that marriage should be only for a man and a woman. Some believe this for religious reasons or because that's the way things have always been done. Others argue that allowing gay and lesbian couples to legally marry would somehow hurt heterosexual family life and heterosexual marriage.

### Are all people against gay marriages?

No. Approximately 34 percent of Americans are in favor of allowing gay people to legally marry (according to a spring 2000 poll), including me. I disagree with all the arguments against allowing gay and lesbian couples to legally marry. Religious beliefs, cultural traditions, and myths are no excuse for discrimination. Committed gay and lesbian couples should have all the same legal privileges and responsibilities enjoyed by heterosexual couples, whether it's called marriage, domestic partnership, or a civil union. Anything less is unfair and discriminatory.

I think the state of Vermont has set a fine example by acting to extend the legal rights of marriage to gay and lesbian couples. But that still leaves forty-nine states where gay and lesbian couples are denied equal rights, so there's still a very long way to go.

### Can gay people have children?

Yes, lesbian and gay people can have children. Many gay men and women, like many heterosexuals, want to be parents. But because two men and two women can't have a baby through sexual relations, gay and lesbian couples who choose to have children do so through a variety of methods, including adoption (except in the handful of states where gay couples are not allowed to adopt).

Also, many gay people who were in heterosexual

marriages before coming to terms with their sexual orientation have children from these relationships. These gay parents often raise their children on their own with a same-gender partner, or jointly with their ex-spouses.

### Will their children be gay, too?

According to all the studies that have been done, children raised by parents who are gay are no more or less likely to be gay or lesbian than children raised by heterosexual parents. They are likely, however, to have a better understanding of gay people.

# chapter 4

# Sex

**What exactly do you mean by sex?**

When I was in college, this was a subject my friends and I usually couldn't agree on. Some people thought that anything you did where you and your partner got sexually excited was sex. Others thought that only sexual intercourse (where a man's penis enters a woman's vagina) was sex and everything else was just fooling around. And still others didn't consider it sex unless you both had an orgasm (an intense feeling of satisfaction and release that you can experience on

75

your own through masturbation or when having sex with another person).

I didn't think any of these definitions worked all that well, especially the penis-in-vagina definition for sex, because that left out gay and lesbian couples entirely. Eventually, I came up with my own definition of what it means to have sex, one that includes all sorts of things that people might do together to give each other sexual pleasure. These include kissing, caressing, cuddling, mutual masturbation (using hands to stimulate each other's genitals), oral sex (using the mouth to stimulate the other person's genitals), sexual intercourse, and anal intercourse (where a man's penis enters his male or female partner's anus). And while many people don't feel they've had sex unless they've had an orgasm, by my definition, an orgasm isn't required for people to have sex.

### Why would two people of the same gender want to have sex with each other?

When two people feel attracted to each other and/or they fall in love, it's perfectly normal for them to want to be physically close, to kiss and touch each other, and to get sexually excited. The urge to have sex is a basic part of the human experience, and it's a very powerful urge. Just as a man and woman can experience these pleasurable feelings, two women or two men can also share these very strong emotional and sexual feelings for each other.

Sometimes a man and woman have sex because they want to make a baby. Since sex between two men or two women can't lead to pregnancy, this isn't a reason for gay or lesbian couples to have sex.

### How do gay and lesbian people have sex? What do they do?

This is, of course, the question that many young people are most curious about. One twelve-year-old girl recently e-mailed me asking if gay people *try* to have sex. I thought for a moment about what she was asking and realized that given what she had learned a few years before in her fourth-grade sexual reproduction class, sex between two men or two women just didn't seem to make sense. Without a penis and vagina, she wondered, how could gay and lesbian couples have sex? Well, if you think of sex only as penis-in-vagina sexual intercourse, then gay and lesbian couples don't have sex. However, by my definition, sex is not limited to vaginal-penile intercourse.

There are many things that gay and lesbian couples do to give each other sexual pleasure. Depending upon what the couple likes to do and what makes them feel good, they may choose to kiss and cuddle, caress each other's body, touch each other's genitals, and engage in oral sex. In addition, some male couples have anal intercourse. The couple may do one or more of these things until each one has an orgasm, although as I noted at the start of this chapter, you can have sex without having an orgasm.

Of course, there are important responsibilities for people to consider even before they begin a sexual relationship. Caring and responsible people take steps to avoid or reduce the risk of getting or passing along a sexually transmitted disease (see the last question in this chapter for more on that subject). And if the couple includes a man and a woman, it's extremely important to know about birth control and to do what's necessary to avoid an unplanned pregnancy.

## Do gay people have sex more often than heterosexual people?

From everything I've read, the average gay man or woman has sex about as often as the average heterosexual man or woman.

However, you will hear some activists who fight against equal rights for gay people claim that gay men have hundreds, even thousands, of sexual partners every year. In spreading this myth, the anti-gay activists hope to turn public opinion against gay people and hurt efforts to extend equal rights to gay men and lesbians. The fact is there are some gay men who have many sexual partners over the course of a weekend, a year, or a lifetime. And the same is true of some heterosexual men as well, but no one would ever argue that heterosexual people don't deserve equal rights because some heterosexual men have many sexual partners.

## Do you have to have sex to know if you're gay or lesbian?

No, you don't. And you don't need to have sex to know if you're heterosexual, either. For the complete answer to this question, please see chapter 1, "The Basic Stuff."

**If you have sex with someone of the same gender just one time, does that make you gay or lesbian? If you have sex with someone of the other gender just one time, does that make you heterosexual?**

When I was a teenager, after I had my first sexual experience with a man and realized I was gay, I decided that I didn't want to be gay. So I figured if I had sex with women that the experience would somehow make me heterosexual. It didn't work. What I discovered, instead, was that trying to have sex with women made me very upset because it wasn't something I really wanted to do; I didn't have feelings of sexual attraction for women and having sex with a woman didn't feel natural to me.

What I didn't understand at that age was that no sexual experience with a man or a woman, whether it's a passionate kiss, mutual masturbation, or sexual intercourse has any impact on whether you're gay, heterosexual, or bisexual. The experience can even be pleasurable, but it makes no difference. That's because your sexual orientation can't be changed by one sexual experience, one hundred sexual experiences, or by prayer, therapy, or anything else.

You may be surprised to learn that some heterosexuals have had homosexual experiences and some gay men and women have had heterosexual experiences. Some people have even learned that they enjoy having sex with both men and women. But while a sexual experience may help you understand what you really feel deep down, as it did for me, no sexual experience has ever changed anyone's true sexual orientation. Your feelings of sexual attraction are yours to keep and enjoy for the rest of your life, but you can't change them.

**I'm a guy and I like being physical with my buddies. I'm a girl and I like being physical with my girlfriends. Does that mean I'm gay?**
That means you're like everybody else, no matter what their sexual orientation. Most human beings like being physical with their friends and with people they care about. It's human nature. That's why people hug, walk arm-in-arm, hold hands, kiss upon greeting, pat each other on the back, and so forth. Being physical or physically affectionate with people you care about is one of the joys of life. Unfortunately, because so many kids are afraid of being thought of as gay, they're more likely today to hold back and not do what comes naturally.

## Do gay men find women physically disgusting?
## Do lesbians find men physically disgusting?

Over the years, it's been rare for me to hear from gay men or from lesbians that they find people of the other gender physically disgusting. It's more a matter of not being interested sexually than being disgusted or turned off.

## If I'm not gay, do I need to worry about AIDS?

Absolutely. Everybody needs to know about the full range of diseases that can be passed from one person to another during sex, including AIDS, which is the most dangerous of sexually transmitted diseases (STDs). And it's important to know about these diseases and how to protect yourself BEFORE you become sexually active.

STDs don't care what your feelings of sexual attraction are. They're just looking for a way to get from one person to another. In the case of AIDS, a potentially deadly disease of the immune system, HIV (the virus that causes AIDS) can be passed from one partner to another during vaginal or anal sexual intercourse, as well as during oral sex. And don't think you can tell just from looking at someone whether he or she has AIDS or any other STD. That's a dangerous myth. A person can look perfectly healthy and still be infected with any number of STDs, including HIV.

### I thought AIDS was a disease that only gay men get? Is that true?

No. When the AIDS virus first appeared in the United States, gay men were among the first to be infected. During the early years of the epidemic, in the 1980s, most of the people who were infected and later died, were gay men. But around the world and more and more in the United States, AIDS is a disease that affects both men and women, regardless of their sexual orientation. In fact, the majority of people worldwide who are infected with the AIDS virus are heterosexual.

### What can people do to keep from getting sexually transmitted diseases?

Sexually transmitted diseases (STDs) can be very dangerous, but they can be prevented. This is something all people need to know about BEFORE they begin engaging in any kind of sexual activity with another person. The many different kinds of sexually transmitted diseases (HIV, syphilis, gonorrhea, and herpes, among others) can be passed from one partner to the other through oral sex, anal sex, and sexual intercourse (penis-in-vagina).

There is only one way to completely avoid sexually transmitted diseases and that is by not doing anything—sexual intercourse, anal sex, and oral sex— where there is the risk of infection. (Keep in mind that it is possible to have a sexual relationship with someone without engaging in these behaviors.)

For people who choose to go beyond kissing and cuddling they can still avoid STDs by using protection, such as condoms or dental dams, when engaging in risky sexual behavior. (Dental dams are protection that's used when engaging in oral sex with a female.) Condoms are effective in preventing most sexually transmitted diseases, as well as unplanned pregnancies, but only if they are used correctly and used every time a person has sexual intercourse.

There is so much more to learn about this subject than what I've been able to say in this brief answer. So, please educate yourself. Talk to your parents, talk to educators and counselors, and consult the resources at the end of this book.

# chapter 5

# God and Religion

**At church, my minister says that homosexuality is a sin. Is that true?**

Many religions and many religious people believe that homosexuality is a sin, but people have all kinds of views on this subject. For example, I don't think homosexuality is a sin. I don't think being gay or lesbian is a sin. And I don't think that having a gay or lesbian relationship is a sin. I also don't believe it's immoral. That's my personal belief and these are the beliefs of many people, including people of all different faiths.

I like what retired Episcopal Bishop John Shelby Spong has to say on this subject. When asked by Parents, Families and Friends of Lesbians and Gays (PFLAG) whether, in his opinion, God regards homosexuality as sin, he answered, "Contemporary research is uncovering new facts that are producing rising conviction that homosexuality, far from being a sickness, sin, perversion, or unnatural act, is a healthy, natural, and affirming form of human sexuality for some people. Our prejudice rejects people or things outside our understanding. But the God of creation speaks and declares, 'I have looked out on everything I have made and behold it [is] very good' (Genesis 1:31). The word of God in Christ says that we are loved, valued, redeemed, and counted as precious no matter how we might be valued by a prejudiced world."

### Does God love gay people?

Yes. I believe that God loves gay people as God loves all people. Again, not everyone agrees with this view. Not everyone believes in God. But, if there is a God, we trust that God is a loving God, and that a loving God would love all of his or her creations.

## What do the different religions have to say about gay people?

Here is a very brief survey of the official views of the major religions in the United States on the subject of homosexuality. Keep in mind that despite stated positions, there is often strong disagreement among the different denominations, different religious leaders, different congregations, and individual members of a congregation when it comes to opinions about homosexuality.

The Episcopal Church lets openly gay people join the denomination and does not consider homosexuality a sin. The Lutherans let openly gay people join, but consider homosexuality a sin and believe that it is not in God's original plan. Presbyterians don't have one voice on this issue, except that openly gay, sexually active people cannot serve as Presbyterian ministers. The Roman Catholic church permits openly gay people to join, but considers homosexuality morally wrong and a sin if practiced. The Baptists officially let openly gay people join and consider homosexuality a sin, but the American Baptists and Southern Baptists differ on their views, and individual churches set their own rules. The United Methodists let openly gay people join and do not officially consider homosexuality a sin. The Mormon Church does not let openly gay people join, considers homosexuality a sin, and recommends chastity for homosexuals.

Muslims do not let openly gay people join, consider homosexuality one of the worst sins, and encourage homosexuals to change. Orthodox Jews believe that homosexuality is an abomination, but the Conservative and Reform movements of Judaism welcome gay and lesbian people to their congregations. The Reconstructionist movement of Judaism ordains gay and lesbian rabbis. Buddhists openly welcome gay people, ordain them, and don't consider homosexuality a sin. The Unitarian Universalist Association welcomes gay men and women in all church roles. And the Universal Fellowship of the Metropolitan Community Churches (UFMCC) extends a special welcome to gay, lesbian, bisexual, and transgender people.

**Doesn't the Bible teach that homosexuality is wrong?**
The Bible does not discuss sexual orientation as we understand it today, although the Bible's "Holiness Code" (Book of Leviticus) bans homosexual acts between men (the Bible says nothing about sex between women). But as Peter J. Gomes, an American

Baptist minister and professor of Christian morals at Harvard University noted in a *New York Times* editorial, "...[the code] also prohibits eating raw meat, planting two different kids of seed in the same field, and wearing garments with two different kinds of yarn. Tattoos, adultery, and sexual intercourse during a woman's menstrual period are similarly outlawed."

While many people continue to draw inspiration from the Bible, most have wisely rejected many of the outdated laws and customs first set down in the Bible centuries ago. And just as Christians have rejected the Bible's teachings as justification for slavery, I think that most Christians will eventually reject the Bible's teachings on homosexuality as an excuse to condemn gay and lesbian people and to deny them equal rights.

### Haven't religious leaders also said good things about gay people?

Yes, and over the years many religious leaders have challenged the official anti-gay rules and teachings of their respective religions. Some religious leaders have worked quietly within their denominations to change anti-gay rules, and others have made very public statements and protests. Some religious leaders have also taken active roles in the gay civil rights effort since it first began in the 1950s.

**What did Jesus have to say about homosexuality?**
Nothing. Despite the many things some Christian religious leaders have said against gay and lesbian people, not one of them was ever attributed to Jesus.

**Can gay people become heterosexual through prayer?**
No. Gay people cannot become heterosexual through prayer. That idea is just as silly as thinking that heterosexuals can become gay through prayer. Still, many parents have encouraged their gay and lesbian children to pray for a "healing." That is exactly what Mary Griffith, who once held Christian fundamentalist beliefs, encouraged her gay teenage son, Bobby, to do. Mary later said that at the time, "We hoped God would heal him of being gay. According to God's word, as we were led to understand it, Bobby had to repent or God would damn him to hell and eternal punishment. Blindly, I accepted the idea that it is God's nature to torment and intimidate us."

So Bobby prayed, all the while fearing he would be punished by God for his homosexuality. He wrote in his diary, "Why did you do this to me, God? Am I going to hell? That's the question that's always drilling little holes in the back of my mind. Please don't send me to hell. I'm really not that bad, am I? I want to be good. I want to amount to something. I need your seal of approval. If I had that, I would be happy. Life is so cruel and unfair."

A year and a half after this diary entry, still tormented by guilt and despondent over his unanswered prayers, Bobby jumped off a highway overpass and landed in the path of an eighteen-wheel truck.

In a letter to gay young people printed in the *San Francisco Examiner*, Bobby's mother wrote, "I firmly believe—though I did not, back then—that my son Bobby's suicide is the end result of homophobia and ignorance within most Protestant and Catholic churches, and consequently within society, our public schools, our own family.

"Bobby was not drunk, nor did he use drugs. It's just that we could never accept him for who he was—a gay person... Looking back, I realize how depraved it was to instill false guilt in an innocent child's conscience, causing a distorted image of life, God, and self, leaving little if any feeling of personal worth. Had I viewed my son's life with a pure heart, I would have recognized him as a tender spirit in God's eyes." (The story of Mary Griffith and her son, Bobby Griffith, is told in the book *Prayers for Bobby*. See "Resources.")

### Are there churches just for gay people?

Yes. The Metropolitan Community Church (MCC), whose membership is primarily gay and lesbian, has more than three hundred congregations in the United States and around the world. The largest of the MCC congregations is the 2,300-member Cathedral of Hope in Dallas.

### Are there other places of worship specifically for gay and lesbian people who are religious?

Yes. For example, most major cities have a gay and lesbian synagogue (for Jewish people). And there are organizations all across the country specifically for gay and lesbian people who are Catholic, Jewish, Episcopal, Lutheran, Muslim, Mormon, and just about any other religious denomination you can name. (See "Resources.")

### If I'm lesbian or gay and my religious beliefs tell me that what I am is wrong, what can I do?

Many people, young and old, have written to me over the years about conflicts between their religious beliefs and their sexual feelings. Often, what they know in their hearts about themselves has clashed harshly with the teachings of their religions. This is a personal challenge for which there is no one answer.

For Mark, who thought he was going to hell because of what his pastor said in church, the personal conflict was enormous. Finally, he came to terms with his sexuality and what his church had taught him. "I was having anxiety attacks every day. There were six to nine months of hell. I couldn't breathe. I remember sitting in church every Sunday feeling very nervous. Then something just snapped in my brain. It was the thought of going to college and planning out my adult life. It was the promise of love. I started imagining this guy I would fall in love with. It was the power of love out there that overpowered the bad feelings. And then I read everything I could about gay people and learned about gay religious groups and that there were people who read the Bible who were gay and were also religious. That did it for me."

Carolyn Mobley also struggled with her sexuality, which she once believed was sinful. But then as a college student she realized that her sexuality was not sinful but, instead, a gift from God. I met Carolyn several years ago, when she was an assistant pastor for the Metropolitan Community Church. I hope that her story, which follows, will help you to think in new ways about what you have been taught and what you know to be true about yourself or about a gay person you know.

Carolyn gives credit to the Reverend Martin Luther King, Jr., with helping her come to terms with being a lesbian. She told me, "Dr. King's commitment to disobeying unjust laws had a profound impact on my thinking. I began to question the things that I was told to do. Are they really right? Are they right if I'm told they're right by a person in a position of authority? I began to realize that parents could steer you wrong. Preachers, God knows, could steer you wrong. They were all fallible human beings; they could make mistakes. That really changed my way of looking at myself and the world. And it certainly helped me reevaluate the message I was getting from the church about homosexuality. It made me examine more closely what the Scripture [Bible] had to say about it."

After examining the Scripture, Carolyn came to the following conclusion: "God didn't deliver me from my sexuality. God delivered me from guilt and shame and gave me a sense of pride and wholeness that I really needed. My sexuality was a gift from God, and so is everyone's sexuality, no matter how it's oriented. It's a gift to be able to love." I couldn't agree more.

# chapter 6

# School

**What is taught at school about gay people?**

**V**ery little, if anything, is taught at most grammar, middle, and high schools about gay and lesbian people, gay history, or gay issues. But there are exceptions. Some schools invite special guests to speak about gay and lesbian issues. Some have shown educational documentaries, including *It's Elementary: Talking about Gay Issues in School,* and *Out of the Past.* Some have public bulletin boards where news stories about gay issues are posted.

Some school libraries have books about the subject. And some individual teachers have included gay and lesbian issues in their regular lessons, usually in the context of English, health, or social studies classes.

Chris Lord, who teaches sixth-grade American history and seventh-grade civics at a private school in Maryland, includes gay and lesbian issues when he thinks it's appropriate. "We do a civil rights movement unit and it's most appropriate to use something current, like the gay rights movement." Chris said that more often than not, the subject comes up as a natural part of class discussions. "For example, in my sixth-grade class, I questioned someone's use of the word 'redneck.' Then we went through a lot of the put-down words people use, and the kids locked on to the word 'faggot.' That led to a thirty-five minute discussion."

One reason Chris thinks that students are comfortable discussing gay issues in his class is that he usually volunteers the fact he has a gay father. Chris told me, "On the wall next to my desk, I have a picture of my dad and his partner." Chris also maintains a bulletin board in his class where news items are posted about gay issues.

## How do kids react to the subject when it comes up in class?

Depending upon the school, the class, the age of the students, and the attitude of the teacher, students may be curious and eager to talk, quietly respectful, embarrassed, confused, or even hostile.

When Erica recently spoke up in her civics class during a discussion about gay civil rights, her twelve-year-old classmates listened quietly and respectfully. It wasn't easy for her to overcome her fear, but she did it. Knowing that her teacher, Chris Lord, has a gay father, helped give her the confidence to say what was on her mind. Erica told me, "I said I thought it was wrong what most kids think and they should learn more about it before they have an opinion. Most kids think being gay is sick and nasty and that gay people have a choice. I just said there's nothing wrong with being gay, that my uncle was gay and he's perfectly fine. My classmates agreed with me that it wasn't wrong."

Jackson can't imagine speaking up in class at his small high school outside Portland, Oregon, especially after a recent incident where a student defended gay people during a class debate. He recalled, "The kids started yelling at him that he was a faggot, and he sort of backed down and said that it wasn't that he liked gay people or anything, but that there wasn't anything wrong with them. There were kids just screaming at him, saying things like 'God created Adam and Eve, not Adam and Steve.' It was kind of getting extreme and I was wondering if the teacher would stop them, but he just sat there and didn't say anything." Jackson didn't say anything either, because he doesn't want anyone to know he's gay and was afraid of drawing attention to himself.

Mae knew she would be drawing attention to herself when she gave a "persuasive speech" in her twelfth-grade English class on the subject of gay people. After ninth grade, when her ex-girlfriend had spread rumors about her being gay, Mae started at a new high school and within a few months after arriving, began telling people that she was gay. By twelfth grade, everybody knew.

When it came time to decide on a topic for her persuasive speech, Mae knew she wanted to do something different from her classmates. "Most people were doing it on abortion or about lowering the drinking age. I wanted to tell everybody what it was like to be gay and why same-sex marriage should be legalized." Still, she was nervous. "Up to this time, nobody had ever said anything to my face that was negative, but I was afraid of the snickering and the whispering. I didn't know how people would react.

"I started by asking how they would like to live in a world where you couldn't marry the man or woman you loved, you couldn't tell your parents about a crush. Then I said that that's how it was for me, for gay people. Everybody was paying attention and it was all eyes on me, including my teacher. She'd been looking down at her papers. Then when I said the word 'gay,' she looked up at me and looked at me dead on. I don't think she expected something quite that different. When I finished, it was kind of silent at first. Most people were shocked that I had the nerve to talk about this. After class, a lot of them told me what a good job I'd done."

### How do parents react to their children being taught about gay and lesbian issues?

Some parents are pleased that the subject is being taught. Others have nothing to say. Some think it's inappropriate or wrong. And some think that anything positive said by a teacher about gay people is grounds for being fired.

## Why do some parents object to teaching students about gay people?

Some parents object to talking about sexuality in any form in schools. Other parents believe that by talking about homosexuality, you will encourage students to become gay. Of course, you can't make anyone gay. But by teaching kids the truth instead of the old negative myths, you can make them better informed, more understanding, and more comfortable with their own sexuality.

Another reason some parents object to teaching children about this subject is that they have strong negative beliefs about homosexuality and gay people. They want to pass these beliefs on to their children and don't want them to hear any other points of view on this subject, especially at school.

## Are there gay and lesbian teachers?

There have always been gay and lesbian teachers, but until recent years, all teachers kept their sexual orientation a secret. This has begun to change, especially at colleges and universities and some high schools. And there are now organizations for gay and lesbian teachers in major cities across the country. But when it comes to middle schools and grade schools, it is rare to find any teachers who are openly gay.

### Why do they keep it a secret?

Gay and lesbian teachers have kept their sexual orientation secret for a number of reasons. Many have feared losing their jobs and/or they've been afraid of negative reactions from their colleagues, administrators, or from parents who object to gay people being teachers. And because relatively few teachers are openly gay, those who are open often find themselves in the position of being pioneers. Charting new territory is never easy, especially when your job may be on the line.

Not many years ago, lesbian and gay teachers whose secret was found out were fired from their jobs and lost their teaching licenses. Now there are laws in many places that protect gay and lesbian people from being fired simply because they are gay, but that depends upon local or state laws or the policy of the school. And even where there are laws protecting gay people from being fired, teachers may still be afraid that their careers could be harmed if it became known that they were gay, especially if they work with young children.

## Why would anyone object to gay and lesbian people being teachers?

Some people mistakenly believe that gay and lesbian teachers will somehow influence their students to become gay. Other people mistakenly believe that gay men and lesbians are more likely to be child molesters. And still others believe that gay people are sinful and immoral, so they think gay teachers are poor role models for children.

## If I'm being teased or called names because I'm gay or because someone thinks I'm gay, is there anyone at school I can talk to?

With any luck, there is a school nurse, counselor, a teacher, or an administrator you can talk to. At some schools, there are administrators, counselors, and/or teachers who put a "Safe Zone" sticker outside their office or classroom, so gay and lesbian students or those who have questions about gay issues will know they are welcome.

If there is no one at your school you think you can talk to and you can't talk to your parents, contact one of the resources listed at the back of this book.

**Are there any school organizations for kids who are gay, think they're gay, or for kids who have friends or family members who are gay?**

Yes. There are more than 700 gay-straight alliances (GSAs) and similar groups at high schools across the country, from New York to Alaska for gay, lesbian, bisexual, transgender teenagers, and their friends and supporters. Some of the groups have been started by gay and lesbian kids, some have been started by heterosexual kids who have gay and lesbian friends or family members, and some have been started by teachers and administrators.

One of the first high school GSAs was started in 1989 at Concord Academy, a private high school in Concord, Massachusetts. A second-year student, whose mother was gay, was upset by all the anti-gay comments she heard around school. So with the hope of changing things at Concord Academy, the student spoke to her history teacher, Kevin Jennings—who happened to be gay—about starting a student group of some kind. They wanted everyone to feel welcome, so together they came up with the name "gay-straight alliance." Since then, through the supporting efforts of Student Pride USA, a program of the Gay, Lesbian & Straight Education Network (GLSEN), the idea has spread like wildfire.

In general, the goal of high school GSAs is to provide a supportive and safe place for open discussion between gay and non-gay students about the issues gay students face in school, with their families, and within their communities. GSAs are open to all students, and no student has to identify his or her own sexual orientation. (For information about finding a local GSA or starting one at your school, contact GLSEN. See "Resources.")

**Are things different once you get to college?**
In most cases, yes, although it depends on the college or university you attend. But in general, at a college or university you're likely to find openly gay and lesbian professors, and gay and lesbian students are likely to find a more welcoming environment than in middle school and high school. There are also at least two dozen colleges and universities that have lesbian and gay studies programs, and more than ninety schools offer at least one course on some aspect of homosexuality. Besides formal courses, college students may first hear about homosexuality during orientation and gay and lesbian issues are likely to come up in a variety of courses from English literature to history.

# chapter 7

# Activism and Discrimination

**Why do gay people have special parades?**

Every June, across the United States and in countries around the world, gay and lesbian people hold parades and festivals. All of these celebrations mark the anniversary of the Stonewall Riot, an important event in the gay civil rights movement.

In the early morning hours of June 28, 1969, the New York City police raided the Stonewall Inn, a gay bar in Greenwich Village. In those days it was routine for the police to harass, arrest, and sometimes beat gay and lesbian patrons at gay bars and clubs. Most often, the bar patrons did their best to avoid trouble and keep from being arrested, because you could lose your job if anyone found out you were gay. But this time, the gay men and lesbians at the bar fought back and that led to a riot. Publicity from this event led to the formation of gay and lesbian civil rights organizations across the country, especially at colleges and universities.

People go to these events for many different reasons. Some heterosexual people go to show their support for gay people in general and some go to show their support for their family and friends who are gay. Some go to demand equal rights for gay people. Some gay people go to have a good time or to show their sense of pride in being themselves. And some gay and lesbian people go so they can be around a lot of other gay people.

I remember the first time I went to a gay pride parade in New York City. It was amazing to see so many gay and lesbian people in one place. And such a variety! It made me feel good about myself to know that I wasn't alone and to see so many gay people who looked happy.

## When did the gay civil rights movement start?

In Germany, gay rights organizations were first started in the late 1800s, but were later wiped out by the Nazis. In 1924, Henry Gerber attempted to start the first gay organization here in the United States, but the U.S. gay rights movement didn't really get going until the 1950s. That's when a handful of men and women very courageously, and successfully, formed a number of different organizations including the Mattachine Society and Daughters of Bilitis. Attitudes towards gay people were very negative in those days and people were afraid to even go to meetings or to use their real names.

At meetings of these groups, people talked about the problems they faced. Some organizations fought for the right of gay and lesbian people to get together at bars without being harassed or arrested by the police. And they also published the first magazines for gay and lesbian people. However, it wasn't until the late 1960s, following the Stonewall Riot in New York City, that the gay civil rights movement became a national force.

**I've heard that gay people want special rights. Don't you agree that no one should have special rights?**

I agree that no one should have special rights. But you'll never hear gay and lesbian people asking for special rights. That's because what gay and lesbian people want is equal rights. They want to work just like everyone else, without worrying about being fired because they're gay. They want to go to school like everyone else, without getting called names or being physically attacked because they're gay. They want the right to get married just like everyone else. They want to be treated equally.

The people who claim that gay men and women want special rights are trying to make you believe that gay men and women want something more than what everyone else has. That's how they get people to vote against laws that protect gay people from discrimination.

I think we can agree that no one deserves special rights. But we can also agree that all people deserve equal rights.

**Aren't gay people already protected by laws that forbid discrimination?**

Yes and no. There are eleven states and many cities

that have laws that protect gay and lesbian people from discrimination. There are companies, colleges and universities that protect gay people from discrimination. And federal employees who are gay are protected by law. But there is no national law that protects gay people from discrimination in the same way that all other Americans are already protected because of their race, religion, age, disability, etc. That's why you hear in the news about people fighting for local, state, and national laws to protect gay people from discrimination.

**How are gay people discriminated against today?**
Things are much better today than when the first group of people started the early gay rights organizations in the 1950s. In those days, gay people didn't even think about being open about their sexual orientation, because anyone who was found out could easily be fired from his or her job, get thrown out of college, be forced to move out of their apartment, or even be committed to a hospital for the mentally ill. And there was nowhere for you to turn when these things happened. There were no gay legal organizations, no anti-discrimination laws, no pro-gay politicians, nothing.

The world has changed a lot for gay people in a half-century, but there are still problems with discrimination; people are still fired because they're gay, and there are many places in the United States where this is legal. Gay and lesbian couples, no matter how many years they have been together, are denied the protections given to heterosexual married couples in every state but Vermont. Gay and lesbian parents are still sometimes denied custody of their children in divorce cases, simply because they're gay. Gay boys are not allowed to join the Boy Scouts. Gay kids are routinely harassed at schools across the country. Some gay-straight alliances have even been forced to go to court to win the right to meet on school grounds. (The Salt Lake City school district voted to ban all non-curricular clubs to avoid having to allow a GSA to meet at one of its high schools.) And gay people are sometimes the targets of violence. Some people are even killed because they're gay, as in the 1998 murder of Matthew Shepard, a student at the University of Wyoming who was tied to a fence, brutally beaten, and left to die.

## Why are lesbian and gay people who serve in the United States military forced to keep their sexual orientation a secret?

That's a good question. If you ask the people in charge of the military why they have these "Don't Ask, Don't Tell" rules, they'll tell you that they believe it would undermine morale and make it hard for soldiers to work as a team if gay people in the military didn't keep their sexual orientation a secret. But that hasn't been the experience in Canada, all western European countries, and Israel. In these countries, gay people in the military are not forced to keep their sexual orientation a secret.

There have been many studies done about this issue, including some conducted by the United States military. All of these studies have shown that military and political leaders who don't want openly gay people to serve in the military are guided by prejudice and myths, not facts.

## How do countries around the world deal with gay and lesbian people?

In some places, gay people are treated no differently from anyone else and can live their lives, for the most part, the same way that heterosexual people do. In others, like Iran, where homosexual acts are illegal for both men and women and are punishable by death, gay people have to be very careful to keep their sexual orientation a secret.

In general, European countries have very liberal attitudes toward homosexuality and gay people are protected by law from discrimination. In other parts of the world, particularly Asia and Africa, gay and lesbian people often face great difficulties. For example, in Zimbabwe, President Robert Mugabe has led a very public anti-gay campaign, calling gay and lesbian people "worse than pigs and dogs," declaring that they have no civil rights. By contrast, South Africa is the first—and currently, the only—country with a constitution that bans discrimination against gay people.

### Are there organizations working for gay kids?

Yes. There are currently about one hundred different organizations across the country that provide a wide range of services for gay, lesbian, bisexual, and transgender youths, from peer counseling to education. These organizations are members of the National Youth Advocacy Coalition (NYAC). In addition to working with many different organizations, NYAC provides all kinds of information directly to kids, through crisis hot lines, publications, and pen-pal groups. (See "Resources.")

Another group that is working very hard for gay kids is the Gay, Lesbian & Straight Education Network (GLSEN). GLSEN has nearly one hundred chapters all across the country with more than 20,000 members. The organization's goal is to make sure that "each member of every school community is valued and respected, regardless of sexual orientation." GLSEN's efforts include helping high school GSAs (gay-straight alliances) and working with education organizations to improve upon what students are taught about homosexuality and gay people.

### What can kids do to make a difference?

Kids can do a lot to make a difference, including speaking up in class as Erica and Mae did, telling friends not to use anti-gay language, asking your teacher to post a news bulletin board for stories on gay and lesbian issues, and starting or joining a GSA (gay-straight alliance).

Six of Chris Lord's students decided to testify at Maryland state hearings in favor of adding sexual orientation to a proposed anti-discrimination and hate crimes bill. Chris told me, "The six girls sat there for seven hours and all of them testified in front of the sub-committee in favor of the bill. They had done their research and did very well. This was an issue they felt strongly about."

And in Orange County, California, a group of students have gone to court to fight discrimination in their own backyard. The Orange Unified School District rejected their application to establish a GSA at El Modena High School. Rather than give up, the students, with the support of their parents, decided to sue.

Kevin is in eleventh grade at a school about an hour from El Modena High. He's the president of his school's GSA, and thinks that one of the most important things for kids to do is to "break the cycle of hate." He explained, "There's a poem called 'Carefully Taught' about how parents teach their children to hate and their children teach their children to hate. If people understand that being gay is okay, that it's perfectly natural, it would be an easier environment for gay people to come out in. It would be better for everyone."

## What does the whole poem say?

It's actually not a poem, but the lyrics from a song, "You've Got To Be Carefully Taught," from the Broadway musical *South Pacific* by Richard Rodgers and Oscar Hammerstein II. The lyrics, which are as true today as they were when Hammerstein wrote them in 1949, talk about the responsibility adults bear for passing prejudice down from one generation to the next. Perhaps your generation will do better than generations past in making the world a more welcoming place for all people, no matter what their differences are.

# Resources

Are you looking for someone to talk to? Help with a problem? Specific information for black, Hispanic, Asian and other minority youth? Ideas on how to start a gay-straight alliance at your school? A telephone number for a gay youth group in your area? A telephone hotline? A book or video? Help with a religious question? Then you've come to the right place. Have a look at some of the books and videos I list; write, call, or e-mail the appropriate organization or spend some time browsing through the organization's website; call a telephone hotline; or log-on to one or more of the youth-oriented websites. All of the information you're looking for is out there, and the resources in this section will help you find it.

## A Warning About The Internet

You'll see that virtually all of the organizations I list have a website. That means if you have access to the Internet, you can get enormous amounts of information and help online. You can also purchase the books and videos I list through a commercial website.

But it is extremely important to be cautious when you use the Internet, especially if you decide to join a discussion group or use the Internet to meet other young people. Because it's so easy to create a false online profile, it can be hard to tell who is being truthful and who is not. So there's the possibility that someone may try to take advantage of you, may make you uncomfortable online, or might try to arrange to meet you when they should not. Always remember that when meeting people online, you should use the same caution you would when meeting any stranger. Never give out your telephone number or home address and never agree to meet anyone in person unless you are accompanied by a parent or another responsible adult, and then only meet in a public place.

The Internet is an amazing resource, but I urge you to be careful and use common sense. And if possible, please seek guidance from your parents or a responsible adult.

## BOOKS

There are relatively few books written specifically for young people with a focus on gay issues or using gay and lesbian themes. And virtually all of these books are written for teenagers, so not all of them are appropriate for younger readers.

*Prayers for Bobby: A Mother's Coming to Terms with the Suicide of Her Gay Son*, by Leroy Aarons. HarperSanFrancisco, 1996. Author Leroy Aarons traces Mary Griffith's struggle to reconcile her teenage son's sexuality, his suicide, and her own religious beliefs. (Not written specifically for young adults.)

*Free Your Mind: The Book for Gay, Lesbian, and Bisexual Youth and Their Allies,* by Ellen Bass and Kate Kaufman. HarperCollins, 1996. *Free Your Mind* offers practical advice and information for young gay, lesbian, and bisexual people as well as their families, teachers, counselors, and friends.

*Am I Blue? Coming Out From the Silence*, Marion Dane Bauer, editor. Trophy Press, 1995. This ALA award-winning anthology includes sixteen funny, sad, and memorable short stories for teens about coming out as gay or lesbian.

**Passages of Pride: Lesbian and Gay Youth Come of Age,** by Kurt Chandler. Times Books, 1995. Six teenagers speak of the challenges they faced growing up, coming out, and making peace at home, school, and on their own.

**Queer 13 : Lesbian and Gay Writers Recall Seventh Grade,** Clifford Chase, editor. Rob Weisbach Books, 1999. Twenty-five stories written by many of the up-and-coming voices in literature provide various points of view about their teen years.

**Joining the Tribe: Growing Up Gay and Lesbian in the '90s,** by Linnea Due. Anchor Books, 1995. Linnea Due offers a compassionate book, which realistically and vividly portrays the challenges faced by gay, lesbian, and bisexual teens.

**Annie On My Mind,** by Nancy Garden. Farrar Straus & Giroux, 1992. Seventeen-year-old Liza's friendship with Annie turns into a love relationship. Once discovered, they must find the strength to stay together.

**Two Teenagers in Twenty: Writings by Gay and Lesbian Youth,** Ann Heron, editor. Alyson, 1994. Forty-two people between the ages of twelve and twenty-four describe how they came to realize they were gay, how they explained their sexual orientation to their families and friends, and how their lives have been affected by their sexuality.

***Becoming Visible: A Reader in Gay and Lesbian History for High School and College Students***, *Kevin Jennings, editor. Alyson, 1994.*
The selections included here cover more than 2000 years of history and a diverse range of cultures. Questions and suggestions for classroom activities follow at the end of each section.

***Does Your Mama Know? An Anthology of Black Lesbian Coming Out Stories***, *Lisa C. Moore, editor. Redbone Press, 1998.*
The complex emotions that accompany coming out are captured in forty-nine short stories, poems, interviews, and essays. (Not written specifically for young adults, but appropriate for high school students.)

***Growing Up Gay/Growing Up Lesbian: A Literary Anthology***, *Bennett L. Singer, editor. New Press, 1994.* More than fifty prominent lesbian and gay writers and scholars have contributed coming of age and coming out stories to this anthology.

***From The Notebooks of Melanin Sun***, *by Jacqueline Woodson. Scholastic, 1997.* A fourteen-year-old African-American boy has to decide what to do when his mother announces she is gay. Winner of the 1996 Coretta Scott King Honor Book Award, Jane Addams Peace Award, and ALA Best Book for Young Adults.

# VIDEOS

*All God's Children*, produced by *Woman Vision, The National Gay and Lesbian Task Force, and The National Black Lesbian and Gay Leadership Forum, 26 minutes, 1996.* All God's Children chronicles the Black Church's acceptance of African-American lesbian and gay people. Includes classroom study guide.

*Both of My Moms' Names Are Judy*, produced by *Lesbian and Gay Parents Association, 11 minutes, 1994.* Children ages 7-11 candidly discuss their families, playground teasing, and classroom silence. Presenter's guide included.

*Gay Youth*, produced by *Pam Walton, 40 minutes, 1995.*
*Gay Youth* details the lives two young people, showing that information, acceptance, and support can make an enormous difference to lesbian and gay youth.

*Growing Up Gay and Lesbian*, 57 minutes, 1993.
Brian McNaught puts a powerful face on the issue with this non-threatening but highly effective presentation on the isolation and alienation of growing up gay. Aired repeatedly on PBS stations nationally, it received the highest rating from the American Library Association.

***I Just Want to Say***, *produced by GLSEN, 13 minutes, 1998.*
A panel of parents, students, and teachers talk about anti-gay bias in schools. Hosted by Martina Navratilova.

***In the Life: Back to School***, *57 minutes, October-November 1997.*
Drawn from the award-winning public television newsmagazine series, this video includes segments on gay-straight alliances, supportive Mormon families, youth suicide, the "Ex-Gay" movement, and gay youth support services around the country.

***It's Elementary***, *by Debra Chasnoff and Helen Cohen, 78 minutes, 1995.* Inspiring footage shot in schools across the country shows real examples of school activities, faculty meetings, and classroom discussions of lesbian, gay, bisexual, and transgender issues. Includes classroom study guide.

***Out of the Past***, *by Jeff Dupre, 60 minutes, 1998.*
Through the eyes of a young woman coming to terms with herself and her place in the world, "Out of the Past" traces the emergence of gay men and lesbians in American history.

***Reaching Out***, *produced by GLSEN Miami, 21 minutes, 1996.*
Contemporary stories of lesbian, gay, bisexual, and transgender youth are matched with stories about the educators who help them.

***Straight From the Heart***, *produced by Woman Vision, 25 minutes,* 1994. This video contains the stories of parents and their journeys to a new understanding of their lesbian, gay, and bisexual children. Includes a classroom study guide.

## NATIONAL ORGANIZATIONS—GENERAL

There are organizations across the country working on different aspects of the gay civil rights movement. The following groups work at the national level and each maintains a website containing information about the work of the organization. Their websites may also include extensive resource listings, on-line newsletters, libraries, and contact information for local organizations.

### GLAAD (GAY AND LESBIAN ALLIANCE AGAINST DEFAMATION)

Since the mid-1980s, GLAAD has worked to make sure that the various media (including television, magazines, newspapers, and film) do a fair and accurate job of portraying gay, lesbian, bisexual and transgender people. GLAAD's website is packed with all sorts of interesting news and information.

### *GLAAD*

150 West 26th St., #503, New York, NY 10001

Phone: 212-807-1700, 800-GAY-MEDIA

Fax: 212-807-1806

Website: www.glaad.org

E-mail: glaad@glaad.org

## HRC (HUMAN RIGHTS CAMPAIGN)

The Human Rights Campaign has more than 300,000 members, making it the largest national lesbian and gay political organization in the country. HRC lobbies the federal government on gay, lesbian, and AIDS issues; educates the public; participates in election campaigns; organizes volunteers; and provides help to state and local groups that work for gay and lesbian equal rights.

### *Human Rights Campaign*

919 18th St., NW, #800, Washington, DC 20006

Phone: 202-628-4160

Fax:  202-347-5323

Website: www.hrc.org

Email: hrc@hrc.org

## LAMBDA LEGAL DEFENSE AND EDUCATION FUND

Lambda takes on a wide range of legal cases concerning the civil rights

### Lambda Legal Defense and Education Fund

120 Wall St., #1500, New York, NY 10005-3904

Phone: 212-809-8585

Fax: 212-809-0055

Website: www.lambdalegal.org

E-mail: lambdalegal@lambdalegal.org

# NGLTF
# (NATIONAL GAY AND LESBIAN TASK FORCE)

NGLTF works with local and state organizations to help them with their efforts in the gay and lesbian civil rights movement. The NGLTF website provides information on its efforts and has links to the websites of organizations around the country.

### NGLTF

1700 Kalorama Road, NW, Washington, DC 20009-2624

Phone: 202-332-6483

Fax: 202-332-0207

TTY: 202-332-6219

Website: www.ngltf.org

E-mail: ngltf@ngltf.org

## LLEGO
## (THE NATIONAL LATINA/O LESBIAN, GAY, BISEXUAL & TRANSGENDER ORGANIZATION)

Since 1987, LLEGO has been working to build and strengthen the national network of latina/o lesbian, gay, bisexual, and transgender community-based organizations. The LLEGO website contains information specifically for youth.

### *LLEGO*

1612 K St., NW, # 500, Washington, DC 20006

Phone: 202.466.8240

Fax: 202.466.8530

Website: www.llego.org

E-mail: Llego@llego.org

## PFLAG
## (PARENTS, FAMILIES AND FRIENDS OF LESBIANS AND GAYS)

PFLAG is a support, education, and advocacy organization with chapters across the United States and around the world. If you would like to talk to an understanding parent or need specific advice on how to deal with your parents, contact your local PFLAG chapter. The PFLAG website contains organization news, useful information, and listings of local chapters.

*PFLAG*

1726 M St., NW, #400, Washington, DC 20036

Phone: 202-467-8180

Fax: 202-467-8194

Website: www.pflag.org

E-mail: info@pflag.org

# NATIONAL ORGANIZATIONS—YOUTH

There are hundreds of local groups and organizations across the country for gay, lesbian, bisexual, transgender youth, and their allies. The organizations I've listed below are some of the national groups (including one that is specifically for the children of gay and lesbian people). If you want to locate a group in your area, check out the websites of these organizations and also have a look at the listings under "Websites," later in this "Resources" section.

## COLAGE (CHILDREN OF LESBIANS AND GAYS EVERYWHERE)

COLAGE is a support and advocacy organization for daughters and sons of lesbian, gay, bisexual, and transgender parents. The website includes an online newsletter and discussion lists.

### *COLAGE*

3543 18th St., #17, San Francisco, CA 94110

Phone: 415-861-5437

Website: www.colage.org

E-mail: colage@colage.org

## GLSEN (GAY, LESBIAN & STRAIGHT EDUCATION NETWORK)

GLSEN is working to make sure that each member of every school community is valued and respected, regardless of sexual orientation. GLSEN's Student Pride USA program works with gay-straight alliances across the country. The organization's website offers extensive resources for teachers and students, as well as e-mail list-serves and on-line support.

### *GLSEN*

121 West 27th St., #804, New York, NY 10001

Phone: 212-727-0135

Fax: 212-727-0254

Website: www.glsen.org

E-mail: glsen@glsen.org

## GSAS (GAY-STRAIGHT ALLIANCES)

See GLSEN and Student Pride USA

## NATIONAL COALITION FOR GAY, LESBIAN, AND TRANSGENDER YOUTH

See www.outproud.org (in "Websites")

## NYAC
## (NATIONAL YOUTH ADVOCACY COALITION)

The National Youth Advocacy Coalition advocates for and with young people who are lesbian, gay, bisexual, or transgender in an effort to end discrimination. Through NYAC, you can find information on gay youth groups in your area.

### *NYAC*

1638 R St., NW, #300, Washington, DC 20009

Phone: 202-319-7596

Fax: 202-319-7365

Website: www.nyacyouth.org

E-mail: nyac@nyacyouth.org

## STUDENT PRIDE USA

Student Pride USA is a youth-run project that supports, networks, and helps create gay-straight alliances, and similar youth/student groups across the United States. It provides resources, materials, education, trainings, and maintains communications on a daily basis.

***Student Pride*** c/o GLSEN

121 West 27th Street, # 804, New York, NY 10001

Phone: 212-727-0135

Fax: 212-727-0254

Website: www.studentprideUSA.org

E-mail: studentpride@glsen.org

## NATIONAL ORGANIZATIONS—RELIGIOUS

There are religious organizations and groups for gay, lesbian, bisexual, and transgender people in local communities around the country. And there are more than 1,000 congregations from across the religious spectrum that welcome gay and lesbian people. (They are a part of what's called the "Welcoming Congregation" movement.) In this section, you'll find many of the national and umbrella religious groups, most of which provide contact information for local congregations.

### *American Baptists*

## THE ASSOCIATION OF WELCOMING & AFFIRMING BAPTISTS

PO Box 2596, Attleboro Falls, MA 02763-0894

Phone/FAX: 508-226-1945

Website: www.WABaptists.org

E-mail: WABaptists@aol.com

### *Episcopal*
## INTEGRITY
1718 M St., NW, PMB 148

Washington, DC 20036

Phone: 202-462-9193

FAX: 202-588-1486

Website: www.integrityusa.org

E-mail: info@integrityusa.org

### *Jewish*
## WORLD CONGRESS OF GAY, LESBIAN, AND BISEXUAL JEWISH ORGANIZATIONS
P.O. Box 23379, Washington, DC 20026-3379

Phone: 202-452-7424

Website: www.wcgljo.org

E-mail: info@wcgljo.org

### *Lutheran*
## LUTHERANS CONCERNED NORTH AMERICA
(Includes members of all Lutheran denominations in North America)

2466 Sharondale Dr., Atlanta, GA 30305

Phone/FAX: 404-266-9615

Website: www.lcna.org

E-mail: LuthConc@aol.com

*Methodist*

## AFFIRMATION
## UNITED METHODISTS FOR LESBIAN, GAY, BISEXUAL & TRANSGENDERED CONCERNS

P.O. Box 1021, Evanston, IL 60204

Phone: 847-733-9590

Website: www.umaffirm.org

E-mail: umaffirmation@yahoo.com

*Mormon*

## AFFIRMATION

P.O. Box 46022

Los Angeles, CA 90046-0022

Phone: 323-255-7251

Website: www.affirmation.org

(This website contains specific information for Mormon youth.)

*Muslim*

## AL-FATIHA FOUNDATION
## (LGBTQ MUSLIMS & FRIENDS)

405 Park Avenue, Suite 1500, New York, NY 10022

Website: www.al-fatiha.org

E-mail: gaymuslims@yahoo.com

***Roman Catholic***
## DIGNITY/USA
1500 Mass. Ave. NW, #11, Washington, DC 20005-1894

Phone: 202-861-0017

Fax: 202-429-9808

Website: www.dignityusa.org

E-mail: dignity@aol.com

***Unitarian Universalists Association***
## UNITARIAN UNIVERSALISTS OFFICE FOR LESBIAN, GAY, BISEXUAL, AND TRANSGENDER CONCERNS
25 Beacon Street, Boston, MA 02108

Phone: 617-742-2100, ext. 475

Fax: 617-742-0321

Website: www.uua.org/obgltc

E-mail: obgltc@uua.org

***Universal Fellowship of Metropolitan Community Churches (MCC)***
## UNIVERSAL FELLOWSHIP OF METROPOLITAN COMMUNITY CHURCHES
8704 Santa Monica Blvd., 2nd Fl.

West Hollywood, CA 90069-4548

Phone: 310-360-8640

Fax: 310-360-8680

Website: www.ufmcc.com

E- mail: info@ufmcchq.com

## WEBSITES

(See my warning about the Internet at the start of the "Resources" section.)

In addition to the websites maintained by the many organizations I've already listed, I'm including in this section a handful of websites specifically for young people who are interested in gay and lesbian issues and/or are looking for other young people to talk with online. All of these sites have something valuable to offer, but I found www.YouthResource.com to be the most complete.

Just one final warning, please exercise caution and good judgement when accessing the websites that follow. *Some sites may direct you to other websites that I don't necessarily recommend or endorse.*

## WWW.COLAGE.ORG

See "Organizations—Youth"

## WWW.GLSEN.ORG

See "Organizations—Youth"

## WWW.OUTPROUD.ORG

!OUTPROUD! is the website for the National Coalition for Gay, Lesbian, Bisexual, and Transgender Youth. The site offers a wide range of resources to young people and educators, including informational brochures, message boards, and coming out stories. !OUTPROUD! also publishes the QueerAmerica database (see below).

## WWW.QUEERAMERICA.COM

Just type in the first three numbers of your local phone number and the first three numbers of your zip code and the QueerAmerica database will provide a list of all the gay, lesbian, and bisexual resources in your area, including community centers, support organizations, PFLAG chapters, youth groups, and more. Other search alternatives offer access to organizations across the country.

## WWW.STUDENTPRIDEUSA.ORG

See "Organizations—Youth"

## WWW.YOUTH-GUARD.ORG
## WWW.ELIGHT.ORG

These two websites are run by Youth Guardian Services, Inc., a youth-run non-profit organization that provides support services on the Internet to gay, lesbian, bisexual, transgender, questioning, and straight supportive youth. The site offers e-mail discussion groups for different age categories.

## WWW.YOUTHRESOURCE.COM

Of all the websites for youth, YouthResource.com is the most complete. Maintained by Advocates for Youth, a national organization based in Washington, D.C., this site offers online brochures, specific information for youth of color, advice on how to explore the Internet and chat online, recommended videos and books, information on HIV, news, list-serves for different age groups (once you subscribe you can participate in discussions), and advice on how to start a gay-straight alliance at your school.

## TELEPHONE HOTLINES

COUNSELING, INFORMATION, REFERRALS

### 888-THE-GLNH (888-843-4564)

Gay & Lesbian National Hotline

Monday-Friday, 6:00-10:00 p.m., EST

Saturday, noon-5:00 p.m., EST

Peer counseling, general information, and referrals.

Website: www.glnh.org

E-mail: glnh@glnh.org

### 800-347-TEEN (800-347-8336)

Indiana Youth Group Gay, Lesbian, Bisexual Youth Hotline

Friday and Saturday, 7:00–10:00 p.m., EST

### 800-96-YOUTH (800-969-6884)

LYRIC Youth Talkline

Monday-Saturday, 6:30-9:00 p.m., Pacific Time

Peer counseling for gay, lesbian, bisexual, transgender, and questioning youth (ages 23 and under). LYRIC counselors have experience dealing with a range of issues, including coming out, suicide, drug and alcohol addiction, eating disorders, health, and harassment.

## CRISIS INTERVENTION

### *800-850-8078*

TrevorLine Crisis Intervention for Lesbian, Gay, Bisexual, and Transgender Youth

7 days-a-week, 24 hours-a-day

Trained peer counselors are available for gay, lesbian, bisexual, and transgender youth (up to age 25) who are in a crisis and/or are thinking about suicide.

Website: www.trevorproject.com

## AIDS

### *800-342-AIDS*

National AIDS Hotline

Centers for Disease Control

7 days-a-week, 24 hours-a-day

In addition to answering your questions over the telephone, you can request free written information on AIDS and prevention, as well as referrals to local health facilities for testing and treatment.

## SEXUALLY TRANSMITTED DISEASES

### *800-227-8922*

STD Information Line

Centers for Disease Control

7 days-a-week, 24 hours-a-day

In addition to answering your questions over the telephone about sexually transmitted diseases, you can request free written information on STDs and prevention, as well as referrals to local health facilities for testing and treatment.